Thought to Exist

IN THE WILD

Orangutan, *Pongo ponginae:* Islands of Borneo and Sumatra

Thought to Exist

IN THE WILD

Awakening from the Nightmare of Zoos

WRITTEN BY DERRICK JENSEN

PHOTOGRAPHS BY KAREN TWEEDY-HOLMES

Softbound Edition: ISBN 978-0-9728387-1-9
Hardbound Edition: ISBN 978-0-9728387-2-6

Library of Congress Control Number: 2007921397
First Edition 2007

Quotation Credit:
page vii, © 1982 by Stephen Mitchell. Reprinted from *The Selected Poetry of Rainer Maria Rilke,* edited and translated by Stephen Mitchell, by permission of Random House, Inc.

Author portrait by Karen Tweedy-Holmes
Photographer portrait by Diana Naspo

Design and production by Prism Photographics, Inc.,
Santa Cruz, CA — Printed in Singapore

Quantity discounts for purchase of this book are available to animal advocacy, wildlife, environmental and educational organizations, as well as to individuals wishing to give copies as gifts or donations. Photographs from the book are also available for purchase. For more information, contact the publisher.

College professors may order examination copies of No Voice Unheard titles for a free six-month trial period. To order, fax on school letterhead to (831) 479-3225.

NO VOICE UNHEARD

P.O. Box 4171
Santa Cruz, CA 95063
(831) 440-9574
info@novoiceunheard.org
www.NoVoiceUnheard.org

ALSO BY DERRICK JENSEN

THE PANTHER

In the Jardin des Plantes, Paris

His vision, from the constantly passing bars,
has grown so weary that it cannot hold
anything else. It seems to him there are
a thousand bars; and behind the bars, no world.

As he paces in cramped circles, over and over,
the movement of his powerful soft strides
is like a ritual dance around a center
in which a mighty will stands paralyzed.

Only at times, the curtain of the pupils
lifts, quietly—. An image enters in,
rushes down through the tensed, arrested muscles,
plunges into the heart and is gone.

Rainer Maria Rilke
Translated by Stephen Mitchell

Siberian tiger (Amur tiger), *Panthera tigris altaica:*
Amur-Ussuri region of eastern Russia, Manchuria, North Korea

The bear takes seven steps, her claws clicking on concrete. She dips her head, turns, and takes three steps toward the front of the cage. Again she dips her head, again she turns, again she takes seven steps. Another dip, another turn, another three steps. When she gets to where she started she begins all over. Then she does it again. And again. And again. This is what's left of her life.

Outside the cage, people pass by on a sidewalk. Strollers barely come to a stop before their drivers realize there's nothing here to see. They move on. Still the bear paces. Seven steps, head dip, turn. A pair of teenagers approach, wearing walkmans and holding hands. One glance inside is enough, and they're off to the next cage. Three steps, head dip, turn.

My fingers have wrapped themselves tight around the metal railing outside the enclosure. I notice they're sore. My breath catches in my throat. Still the bear paces. I look at the silver on her back, the concave bridge of her nose. Seven steps, head dip, turn. I wonder how long she's been here. A father and son approach, do not stop to stand next to me. Three steps, head dip, turn.

I release the rail, turn, and as I walk away I hear, slowly fading, the rhythmic clicking of claws on concrete.

A zoo is a nightmare taking shape in concrete and steel, iron and glass, moats and electrified fences. It is a nightmare that, for its victims, has no end save death.

Zoo director David Hancocks writes: "Zoos have evolved independently in all cultures around the globe."[1]

Many echo this statement, but it isn't quite true. It is the equivalent of saying that the divine right of kings, Cartesian science, pornography, writing, gunpowder, chainsaws, backhoes, pavement, and nuclear bombs have evolved independently in all cultures around the globe.[2] Some cultures have developed some of these, and some have not. Some cultures have developed zoos, and some have not. Human cultures existed for scores of thousands of years prior to the first zoo's appearance about 4,300 years ago in the Sumerian city of Ur,[3] meaning zoos did not evolve in these cultures. And in the time since the first zoo, thousands of cultures have existed—some to this day (until the dominant culture finishes eradicating them)—with no zoos or their equivalents to be found.

Zoos have, however, evolved in many cultures, from ancient Sumer to Egypt to China to the Mogul Empire to Greece and Rome on up the lineage of Western civilization to the present. But these cultures share something not shared by indigenous cultures such as the San, Tolowa, Shawnee, Aborigine, Karen, and others who did not or do not maintain zoos: they're all civilized.

The change of just one word makes Hancocks' sentence true: "Zoos have evolved independently in all *civilizations* around the globe." As Michael H. Robinson, director of the National Zoo, wrote, "The period of civilization accounts for perhaps 1 percent of our history as hominids. With civilization came urbanization. Shortly after we had developed cities on a grand scale, zoos and botanical gardens sprang up in countries as far apart as Egypt and China."[4]

Civilizations are ways of life characterized by the growth of cities.[5] Cities destroy natural habitat and create environments inimical to the survival of many wild creatures. By definition cities separate their human inhabitants from nonhumans, depriving them of routine, daily, neighborly contact with wild creatures, which until the onset of civilizations—for 99 percent of our existence—was central to the lives of all humans, and to this day remains central to the lives of the noncivilized.

If it can be said that we are the relationships we share, or at least that relationships form us, or at the very least that they influence who we are, how we act, and how we perceive, then the absence of this fundamental daily bond with wild nonhuman others will change who we are, how we perceive wild creatures, how we perceive our role in the world around us, and how we treat ourselves, other humans, and those who are still wild.

Many ancient zoos contained tremendous numbers of animals. Egyptian zoos held thousands of monkeys, wild cats, antelopes, hyenas, gazelles, ibex, and oryx.[6] Some zoo historians suggest that because the creatures in these zoos were considered sacred they were treated well, but as Hancocks points out, "Deification of a species... brought dubious honor. Used in ritualistic sacrifices, sacred ibis, falcons, and crocodiles were mummified by the hundreds of thousands in sanctified ceremonies. The temple slaughters were so great they led to extermination of these species in many parts of Egypt."[7] The Chinese, too, built large zoos, as did princes in India: the Mogul Akbar had five thousand elephants, one thousand camels, and one thousand cheetahs in his collection.[8] The Aztecs' aviary and zoo in Tenochtitlán was large enough to require almost three hundred keepers just for the ducks, fish, and snakes, and three hundred for the rest of the animals. Five hundred turkeys per day were fed to captive eagles and hawks.[9]

Zoo animals have been kept as pets, as oddities, as objects of study, and as entertainment, but mainly—and this is as true today as it was in ancient times—as symbols of prestige and power.

It's not entirely accurate for me to say that ancient zoos contained "tremendous numbers" of animals, just as it wouldn't be entirely accurate for me to say that zoos today contain "tremendous numbers" of animals. Zoos don't contain numbers at all. They contain animals, individuals one and all.

Unfortunately, most of us by now have been to enough zoos to be aware of the stereotype of the creature who has been driven insane by confinement. The bear pacing a precise rectangle, the ostrich incessantly clapping his bill, the elephants rhythmically swaying, swaying, swaying. But the bear I described is no stereotype. She is a bear. She is a bear who like all other bears at one time had desires and preferences all her own, and who may still beneath the madness.

Or at this point she may not.

I walk by a pond. It's a brisk fall day, and I'm wearing many layers. In the sun it's warm, but in the shade dew still clings to blades of grass and pools in the tiny hollows of curved leaves. Spiderwebs shine. Gnats fly in widening circles. Banded wooly bears wet with dew trundle along open ground, or climb grasses chosen over other grasses for reasons known only to them. The pond is calm, and covered with tiny hemlock seeds blown down—released—in last night's windstorm. The seeds cluster around cascara leaves and fletched redwood twigs. Backstriders patrol beneath the surface, and deep below I can see the season's first sacks of frog eggs. They're attached to dead branches I threw in two years ago because I knew the frogs would like them.

I come back inside to work on this book, and I think again of the bear I saw at the zoo. I think I know—and I think you do, too—what she is doing at this precise moment. She is taking seven steps, dipping her head, and turning. She is taking three steps, dipping her head, and turning.

ONE OF THE GREAT DELIGHTS of living on this land is getting to know my neighbors—the plants, animals, and others who live here—as they introduce themselves to me in their own time, on their own terms. The bears, for example, weren't shy, showing me their scat immediately and their bodies soon after, standing on hind legs to put muddy paws on windows and look inside, or showing glimpses of furry rumps that disappeared quickly whenever I approached on a path through the forest, or walking slowly like black ghosts in the deep gray of pre-dawn. Though I am used to them being so forward, it is always a gift when they reveal themselves even more, as one did recently when he took a swim in the pond in front of me.

Robins, flickers, hummingbirds, and phoebes all present

themselves, too. Or rather, like the bear, they present the parts of themselves they want seen. I see robins often, and a couple of times I've seen fragments of blue eggshells long after the babies have left, but I've never seen their nests. It's the same with the others.

These encounters—these introductions—and so many more are always on terms chosen by those who were on this land long before I was: they choose the time, place, and duration of our meetings. Like my human neighbors, and like my human friends, they show me what they want of themselves, when they want to show it, how they want to show it, and for that I am glad. To demand they show me more—and this is as true for nonhumans as it is for humans—would be unconscionably rude. It would be arrogant. It would be abusive. It would destroy the others' trust. It would destroy any potential our relationship may once have had. It would be downright unneighborly.

This presumes I'm interested in relationships. If I were more interested in control than relationships, I might act differently.

Zoos are about power. And, as even one pro-zoo author (and almost all zoo authors are, unfortunately, pro-zoo authors) writes, "You show power by keeping an animal captive; how much more powerful are you if you kill it?"[10]

Entertainment has always been central to the functioning of zoos. In ancient Rome, this often took the form of mass slaughter of animals. Beginning in about the third century BCE, Romans forced captured bull elephants to fight in public arenas. Soon after, gladiators began fighting bulls, a practice that continues to this day in some countries. Within a couple of hundred years Roman generals figured out how to kill, as it were, two birds with one stone—how to keep discipline among the ranks of the military and provide public entertainment—by throwing army deserters into pits to be torn apart by wild animals.[11]

Around 170 BCE the Roman Senate tried to outlaw these various spectacles, not out of concern for animals (including human animals) but as a means of "preventing their plebian political opponents from buying votes through the sponsorship of such popular events."[12] Their attempt at legislation failed.

One problem with spectacles—where more or less passive consumption of entertainment stands in for direct participation in events that affect one personally—is that spectacles substitute vicarious for direct experience and superficial identification for real relationship. Because spectacles are discrete packets of excitement that remain external to audience members, they are functionally incapable of providing consumers with a meaningful, lasting sense of emotional involvement or satisfaction. This is in contrast to real relationships and personal experience, which aren't functionally incapable of providing this sense. Because individuals are infinitely complex, and because real relationships provide infinite opportunities for exploration and discovery—meaning they need not become boring—and because spectacles are by their very nature distant and superficial—meaning that with repetition they will become boring—spectacles must ratchet up their titillation in order to stave off inevitable boredom. They must keep people believing that they have experienced something, even if this belief lasts only for the short time of the spectacle itself. What once was daring becomes banal, then downright dull.

Because of this, the Roman slaughter grew ever more intense over time. To provide just one example among far too many, in 55 BCE the Roman consul Pompey acquired twenty-one elephants from Egypt, promising that they would not be injured. It should surprise none of us that he lied. As a finale to his festival of violence, Pompey had them publicly tortured: "The gladiators killed the elephants slowly, spearing them with javelins, the beasts flailing their great tusks, falling to their knees, trumpeting and wailing fiercely."[13] A few years later, 3,500 animals were killed in twenty-six spectacles ordered by Caesar Augustus. And things keep getting worse: just one event during the reign of Caligula saw the killing of four hundred bears and four hundred animals from Africa. Nero flooded an entire arena so that gladiators could spear seals from boats.[14] Historian W.E.H. Lecky commented, "Simple combat became at last insipid, and every variety of atrocity was devised to stimulate the flagging interest. At one time a bear and a bull, chained together, rolled in fierce combat across the sand; at another, criminals dressed in the skins of wild beasts were thrown to bulls, which [sic] were maddened by red-hot irons, or by darts tipped with burning pitch…. In a single day, at the dedication of the Colosseum by Titus, five thousand animals perished. Under Trajan, the games continued for one hundred and twenty-three successive days. Lions, tigers, elephants, rhinoceroses, hippopotami, giraffes, bulls, stags, even crocodiles and serpents were employed to give novelty to the spectacle. Nor was any form of human suffering wanting…. Ten thousand men fought during the games of Trajan. Nero illumined his gardens during the night by Christians burning in their pitchy shirts. Under Domitian, an army of feeble dwarfs was compelled to fight…. So intense was the craving for blood that a prince was less unpopular if he neglected the distribution of corn than if he neglected the games."[15]

That's not far different from today. We still live more in spectacles than in our own lives. People will suffer degradation and toxification of their total environment—and of their own bodies—with remarkably little resistance, but destroy the televisions and there would be rioting in the streets almost immediately. And while we no longer slaughter animals for entertainment, we should consider the even more egregious horrors of factory farming and the assembly lines of factory slaughterhouses. We should consider that 90 percent of the large fish in the oceans have been killed by this culture, that the great apes and the great cats will most likely soon be extinct. We should consider that this culture is destroying the wild everywhere at an ever-increasing pace. We should consider that this culture is killing the planet.[16] If this culture has evolved in its treatment of nonhumans, the direction of that evolution should not make us proud.

Zoos remain a deadly business. We've all heard the litany of animals killed by abusive patrons; of deer beaten to death by visitors who climbed the fence to get at them; of sea lions stoned to death; of sea lions blinded by cherry bombs; of giraffes stabbed by pitchforks; of the routine poisonings of captive animals; of the sticks, rocks, and other weapons wielded by those who enact the phrase quoted above: "You show power by keeping an animal captive; how much more powerful are you if you kill it?"[17] And we all know that when these animals fight back, it is not their tormenters who get shot.

A century ago a supervisor at the Moscow zoo stated in language equally applicable today, "All day long, an immense crowd, rowdy and bothersome, filed past the cages. This multitude, which would have been seized by mortal panic at the distant sight of any one of these animals at liberty, took great delight in seeing them thus disarmed, humiliated and debased. They took revenge for their own cowardice by deriding them, heckling them in loud voices, and shaking their chains, and the keepers' remonstrations would come up against an unanswerable argument: 'I've paid.'"[18]

The killing of animals is not at issue here; life feeds off life.[19] It always has, and always will. At issue here is relationship. One reason indigenous cultures do not kill their landbases is that they recognize and participate in the fundamental predator/prey relationship: when you consume the flesh of another you take responsibility for the continuation of the other's community.[20] In addition, you are bound to respect the other and to give thanks for the life it gave to sustain yours, in full recognition that someday it will be your turn to give your life to sustain someone else.

One reason civilizations destroy their landbases—and one reason the current global civilization is killing the entire planet—is that as a whole they do not recognize and participate in this relationship: they neither respect nor take responsibility for nonhuman (or for that matter human) communities.

The truth is, civilizations don't much recognize or participate in relationships at all, especially with nonhumans.

ZOO PROPONENTS OFTEN CLAIM that animals in zoos live longer than those in the wild. These claims are repeated endlessly by the mainstream media. Setting aside for a moment the question of whether you'd rather live in a cage or free in your natural community, the claim is an outright lie. The model for this particular statistical sleight of hand was developed in the 1930s and is followed to this day. It ignores the extremely short average lifespan of animals in zoos and discusses only the lifespans of those rare few who live the longest, then presents these ages as though they are average lifespans or something else equally statistically meaningful. This makes it possible to highlight those apes who live twenty, thirty, or fifty years, and to leave unsaid any messy statistics showing that three-quarters of them die before twenty months of captivity.[21]

Zoos are deadly, with "stock turnover" of between one-fifth and one-quarter of the animals per year. "Theoretically," historians Eric Baratay and Elisabeth Hardouin-Fugier note, "zoos could be closed just by calling a halt to their supply of animals for four to six years; at the end of that time, only a few veterans would remain."[22] They also state, "In actual fact, the extreme mortality of wild animals in zoos has always been the driving force behind the massive scale of importations."[23]

We often hear of valiant attempts by zookeepers to breed endangered species such as, for example, pandas, yet we do not so frequently hear that only 21 percent of pandas conceived through artificial insemination and born in Chinese zoos reach even the age of three.[24] Similarly, the lifespans of porpoises are cut in half by captivity and those of dolphins are reduced by thirty years.[25] Given the realities of living in captivity, I'm not sure if these premature deaths are the worst things that can happen to these creatures.

Zookeepers reading the previous paragraphs would almost undoubtedly exclaim that while zoos might have been maybe kind of just a little bit dangerous in the past (I keep thinking about the death report from a zoo in the 1970s reading "American otter—too decomposed for necropsy," leading me to wonder exactly how long an animal must go missing before anyone notices[26]), modern zoos have become paradises. One zookeeper has gone so far as to claim that fences in zoos are not there to keep animals in, but rather to keep *out* all those animals desperately

clamoring to get *in*.[27] But all of this, too, is misleading at best. Extensive studies show that the mortality rate has remained remarkably consistent over the decades. Indeed, graphs showing mortality in the late twentieth century closely match those from the early nineteenth: "In all instances, mortality remained high during the first eighteen months, the principle difference being the presence of a few veterans among twentieth-century animals."[28]

TODAY THE *SAN FRANCISCO CHRONICLE* ran an article entitled, "Bad girls have a good day as they go outside at zoo: Montana grizzlies entertain public, astound keepers." It's a follow-up on a front-page story a couple of days ago entitled, "Nice Grizzly Grotto Poses a Bear of a Problem." That article was about the difficulties faced by the San Francisco Zoo as it designs a cage—oh, sorry, the accepted term these days, and I swear I'm not making this up, is a "habitat"—for a pair of orphaned sister grizzly bears from Montana.

These were the third and fourth articles written about the zoo's acquisition of the bears. The first two articles had similarly sophomoric titles, far too disrespectful for the subject matter: the permanent incarceration of two animals. The first headline read, "Mischievous grizzly cubs to be adopted by S.F. Zoo," and the second: "Rowdy gals face a tamer S.F. lifestyle."

The articles are as disrespectful as their headlines. One article begins, "Downsized but not dead. Food and shelter but no more wild nights. Those will be the trade-offs for two girl grizzlies moving from the vastness of Montana to the San Francisco Zoo. It is, for sure, a radical change in lifestyle." Today's began, "Two grizzly bears from Montana came out of the ursine closet Wednesday at the San Francisco Zoo and immediately went back in." Another not atypical line: "Now, like much of San Francisco, they're facing housing issues."

Have you ever noticed that corporate journalists seem incapable of writing about human-caused suffering or even extirpation of wild animals without derision? I can't tell you how many articles I've seen (buried in the back of the paper) about the worldwide crisis of amphibian extinction with titles like "Frogs croaking: scientists stumped."

All of the articles present the zoo in an altruistic light. The one article that did not begin flippantly ran, "The San Francisco Zoo is rescuing two grizzly bear orphans that [sic] the state of Montana had sentenced to death." This naturally leads to the question of what the bears did that led the state to do this.

The reporter talked to Stella Capoccia, director of the state agency responsible for imposing and executing the death sentence. The bears evidently "got into a barn and foraged on grain a couple of times. Locking the barn didn't work—they had received a food reward and figured it made sense to return. Then last week, Capoccia said, they damaged some property."

When nonhumans damage human property, they are sentenced to death.

Another article gives more details on the property destruction, which the articles call "running amok" and "ransacking": "For starters, the sisters opened the door to a calving shed and consumed 150 pounds of corn. A few weeks later, they broke into a barn.

"'They just raised havoc,' [Terri] Tews [who lives on the ranch] said. 'They flung things around, chewed on a 4-H banner, flattened a plastic garbage can.'

"The next day, they stripped some boards from the barn's exterior. Then they moved to the front yard, crunching bird feeders, digging up carrots, knocking a birdbath off its pedestal and tearing 50-pound feed blocks from a flatbed truck. They also wolfed down the Tews's oat crop."

And perhaps their worst sin of all: "'They pooped all over the place,' Tews said."

The articles total more than five thousand words. In all of these five thousand words no mention was made of the fact that the ranch is in grizzly bear habitat (real habitat, not cage-style HABITAT™), nor that grizzly bears were once common and now are imperiled. One article did mention in passing that an unusually harsh spring had made food scarce for the bears. Even this statement, however, did not hint that the encroachment of civilization into the bears' home

had anything to do with the bears' behavior or their need to find food.

The articles also mislead on two counts when they call the bears "orphans" to be "adopted" (read incarcerated) by the zoo. The first is that the word *orphans* conjures up images of helpless waifs who cannot survive without the assistance of some selfless benefactor. Enter the zoo. But the bears are eighteen months old, old enough to live on their own if only their home is not "ransacked" by industrial humans "running amok," doing far more damage than a whole phalanx of bears could even dream of doing.

The second is that two of the four articles fail to mention the cause of their mother's death. She was killed by the state of Montana for fundamentally the same reason her daughters were sentenced to death—later commuted to life without parole—which is that after houses were built in her home and after her native food sources had been degraded, she destroyed some property. The articles that do mention her death each devote to it precisely one sentence, and of course do not nakedly use any word so indelicate as "killed," or "shot," or even "executed." Instead, according to one article, "The sisters lost their mother late last fall when she was humanely destroyed by Montana's wildlife officials."

In the wild, grizzlies generally range over about sixty square miles. For the past month these two bears have been confined to a 450-square-foot cell. "'I was told it's much bigger than what Martha Stewart has,' said zoo spokeswoman Nancy Chan." The zoo's director of animal care [sic] and conservation [sic] noted that the bears had "kind of turned into couch potatoes." He followed this with the remarkable observation, "In quarantine, they spent a lot of time sitting down. They have what you might call flat heinies." Now that they have been found to be clean of parasites and diseases ("They must have been drinking bottled water," Chan said) they have been released into their new cage—sorry, HABITAT™—which is approximately 10,000 square feet.

The small size is of no major concern, according to a keeper at another zoo that uses electrified fences to enclose grizzlies in a one-acre "forest" during the day and has them sleep on tires in concrete dens at night. "Keeper Wendi

Mello said the natural [sic] setting is more tailored to human than ursine sensibilities. 'As people, we think it's got to be green and pretty,' Mello said. 'But concrete grottos are not a problem at all. And a lot of people think "the bigger the better"—but if a bear is being stimulated every day, that can make up for a lack of design. I'm a big believer in enrichment."

Enrichment, in this case, consists of "anything new and different," such as, Mello said, "paper bags and card-board boxes."

Imagine being so bored, living a life so impoverished that you would be eager for the distraction provided by a paper bag or a cardboard box. Anything to stave off the maddening tedium. An orangutan at another zoo spent years carefully placing a scrap of paper atop his head, then removing it to place on the concrete floor, then once again placing it atop his head.

The bears in San Francisco will be similarly blessed. According to today's article, bearkeeper Deb Cano "plans to shower them with 'enrichment' toys eventually—cardboard boxes, spices, CDs with forest and ocean sounds."[29]

According to one article, "The people who run these habitats [sic] are trying to answer the same question. To rephrase Sigmund Freud: What do grizzlies want?"[30]

Well, these zookeeper must not be trying very hard, because the answers they keep coming up with somehow always seem to include concrete cells, paper bags, cardboard boxes, and most important of all, confinement. HABITAT™.

I am not a grizzly, but I can guarantee that this is not what grizzlies want. I don't even have to try very hard to answer the question. You can answer it, too. We all can. They want habitat, not HABITAT™. They want freedom, not cages. They want to be left alone, and when they interact with humans (and others) they want to be respected. They want to be given the courtesy of being allowed to live in their own homes, without those homes being destroyed.

The same as all the rest of us.

I'm sure the sisters would agree.

And who could blame them?

IN A FEW MINUTES I'm going to take a walk in a forest, a real forest, not a FOREST™. For days I've been eating chanterelles, and so I'll look for more of them. Beautiful amanita muscarias popped into full fruiting yesterday. Some are the size of dinner plates. Of course I won't eat them, but they're a gift to look at, and it is a challenge for me to guess who has taken bites out of them. Probably rabbits. Yesterday I checked and again saw the paw and butt prints where the bear slid into the pond: rains have yet to fully erase them. I'll check again, and check also the progress of the frog egg sacks. I'll try to see what new creatures have pooped along the path, and check to see who has started to eat the rat who died a couple of days ago. After all that I'll go talk to my mom (who has not been shot for destroying property) and then I'll wander back through the forest and watch the limbs of redwoods sway and circle in the day's light breeze.

And right now, once again, the grizzly bear I saw at the zoo takes seven steps forward, dips her head, and turns to the left.

A zoo is a nightmare taking shape in concrete and steel, iron and glass, moats and electrified fences. It is a nightmare that, for its victims, has no end save death.

Let's do the math to find out how much the grizzly sisters cost the Tews family. One hundred and fifty pounds of corn at about $6.50 per fifty pound sack is $19.50. I wouldn't be too concerned about the flattened plastic garbage can: plastic is called plastic because it's plastic (Latin *plasticus,* of molding, from Greek *plastikos,* from *plassein,* to mold, form). A bear has, in fact, flattened one of my mom's garbage cans. I bent it back into shape. But let's pretend the bears broke the can. A good new garbage can costs about $25 at your local hardware store. We're up to $45 so far.

Now to the birdfeeders. Let's say there were three at $10 each—now we're up to $75. Next comes the birdbath, which was "knocked off its pedestal." Here's where I begin to suspect that in reporting this "damage" the Tews and the reporter were both pretending they were filing a claim for insurance, listing every little thing that happened and hoping that someone would buy into the notion that the damage was much worse than it actually was. I have experience with bears and birdbaths. I've seen birdbaths lying on the ground, and bearprints in the soil made muddy by the bathwater. It was a trauma for sure. I had to go to all the effort of putting the birdbath back on the pedestal and then going all the way to the house to get a pitcher of water to fill it back up. It's a hard life.

The Tews and the reporter were pulling the same trick by mentioning the carrots being dug up. Before we place a value on the carrots—which is going to be trivial in any case—I want to say two words to you: *Montana*, and *spring*. Have you ever been to Montana? It's cold. It's very cold. And remember, this was a harsh spring. It doesn't take Hercule Poirot to guess the size of the carrots. Given that they're even *mentioning* these losses, I'm guessing the rest of their claims are similarly trivial (I've been around enough ranches to know that replacing a couple of boards will cost nothing more than the four or five nails it takes to pound them back up, along with the bruised thumb you get when you miss the nail). And I'm afraid I can't help them with the emotional loss of the chewed 4-H banner, although I'm sure there are plenty of kids who would be delighted to have a 4-H banner that had been chewed by actual, genuine, honest-to-goodness grizzly bears: think of the prestige during show and tell! The same goes for the poop: imagine a bear actually pooping in the woods! My advice to the Tews would be for them to watch where they step, to have fun looking carefully at the scat to see what the bears have been eating, and to thank the bears for fertilizing the soil.

It was, for the third time, a hard spring. Once the berries, moths (sometimes forty pounds per day), grubs, and grasses came on, the Tews would probably no longer be blessed with visits from these bears. And remember, this damage was done over a few weeks, meaning the bears were probably costing the Tews far less than their satellite TV bill.

Let's do some more math. Let's say the Tews have two children, two in-laws, and two grandchildren. Let's say that all eight of them go to the zoo so they can see some grizzly bears. It will cost them $120 to go through the gate, not including parking, cotton candy, or the plush bears that went on sale the moment the grizzlies arrived at the zoo.

It costs tens of thousands of dollars per year to keep a bear in a zoo. The state of California, which is closing elementary schools in poor districts in Oakland, will pony up $270,000 for the zoo, with which the director may try to add five thousand square feet to the cage. The director is also hoping to get $4 to $7 million in public and private funding to make this part of a larger exhibit that would include underwater views of the cage's pool.

And, we can ask again, what would these grizzlies want?

It would have been far cheaper and more enjoyable for all concerned had the Tews considered the corn a very small price they pay for the privilege and joy of seeing the grizzly bears—a privilege and joy that ours may very well be the last or next to last generation ever to experience—and had they considered the birdfeeders an even smaller price they pay as rent for living on land that has belonged to grizzly bears since long before the Tews's ancestors came to this continent, and had they considered the garbage can a price they pay as utterly insufficient reparations for the damage they cause to the bears' home (to the "ransacking" and "running amok," as I'm certain the bears would describe it). Instead of calling one of the state's mobile killing units (for that's what those departments of animal control really are), Terri Tews should have said, "Junior, come here." Then she should have taken her grandchild by the hand, led him to the window, showed him the bears, and marveled with him at how glorious it is to be alive.

She did not do that.

We all know why.

If you see an animal in a zoo, you are in control. You can come, and you can go. The animal cannot. She is at your mercy, and at the mercy of those like you. The animal is on display for you.

In the wild, the creature is there for her own purposes. She is not under your control. She can come, and she can go. So can you. Neither of you is on display, and both of you can display as much of yourselves to the other as you wish. It is a meeting of equals.

And that makes all the difference in the world.

I'm always amazed at the number of people who live in the country and then complain about or kill the animals who live there. If you don't like animals and the inconveniences they can bring, don't move into their home.

A big mother bear has been coming around my mom's house for a couple of years. My mom diligently pays her rent to the creature, as she pays her rent to all the others who own this land. She leaves out apples and corn for the bear, peanuts for the squirrels, sugar water for the hummingbirds, and birdseed for the birds, foxes, and the bear. You can always tell when the opossum has been there because he poops in the pan when he's done eating (at least I hope it's when he's done eating). And you can tell when the bear's been there because the pan has been licked clean.

Recently my mom had a bear problem. The mother bear in my mom's neighborhood had a son who was especially curious, or, as those in animal control organizations would say, was running amok. The little bear climbed her porch (she awoke one night to look out and see his furry butt pressed up against her window, giving her the bear equivalent of a moon shot). He knocked her birdbaths off their pedestals. He flattened her garbage can. He bit holes in plastic pitchers. He broke off the top of one of the young apple trees, either not knowing or not caring that I planted them primarily for his grandchildren. But what made her most angry was when he pulled down her hummingbird feeders and chewed holes in their bases. He didn't bother to drink the sugar water—he was just having fun. *Now* she had a bear problem. Her first solution? She called the birdfeeder company and bought some extra bases. No big deal. But soon enough she got tired of replacing those almost every day, and decided to take drastic action. The next time she saw him ambling toward her birdfeeders, she stepped out on her porch and scolded him, just as she would one of her own children. "Don't do that! You already ate your own food off the pan. That's for someone else." The young bear looked at her for a moment, then turned and began to walk away. My mom went inside. The bear stopped, looked over his shoulder, hesitated, thought, then turned again toward the birdfeeders. My mom stepped again outside, and said, in a voice I heard once or twice as a child, "Don't even think about it. If you touch those birdfeeders, there'll be no more birdseed for you." The bear walked into the forest. He returns often, but never again has he touched her birdfeeder, birdbath, pitchers, or anything but the pan of birdseed.

His mother was probably thinking, "How'd you do that? He never listens to *me*."

Years ago I lived in a neighborhood sometimes visited by a bear and her two cubs. All of us humans made an agreement that none of us would call Fish and Game, because we knew if we did, she'd be a dead bear and her cubs would be pacing rectangles in the Spokane Zoo. Most of us left our occasional offerings of food, and she and her cubs occasionally came by to eat them. Those who didn't want to give anything made minor modifications to their lifestyles: not leaving out garbage with food in it, taking down birdfeeders in the spring when the bears were extra hungry, keeping dog food secured. We were all one big happy neighborhood.

Now, I know we've all been told that a fed bear is a dead bear, that animals must never lose their fear of humans. But who are the people who tell us that? Bingo. The same people who *turn* fed bears into dead bears, and who do the same for plenty of other animals besides. A fed bear is nothing more than a fed bear—just as a fed squirrel is a fed squirrel and a fed goldfinch is a fed goldfinch. A bear who's had the misfortune to encounter employees from Animal Control, Department of Wildlife, Department of Fish and Game—or whatever else a government calls the organization—is a dead bear.

To be clear: if you care at all about animals, never, ever report any animal to governmental organizations.[31] These organizations will use nearly any excuse to kill wild animals. Across the whole state of Montana, for example, each year grizzlies kill a few cows, between ten and a hundred sheep, a few other pets or livestock, and they knock over some beehives. That's across the whole state. Not a big problem. Yet for each of these sins grizzlies are killed or imprisoned.

Montana recently killed a grizzly for killing a few chickens. There are fewer than a thousand grizzly bears in the lower forty-eight United States, relegated to about 2 percent of their range prior to the arrival of civilization.

The grizzly bear sisters now in the San Francisco Zoo will spend the rest of their lives in a cage because they caused well under a hundred dollars damage to the property of someone living on their home. This culture's value system is insane.[32]

I am fully aware that even a young bear can kill me. I am also fully aware that humans have lived comfortably side by side with bears and other wild animals for tens of thousands of years. Nature is not scary. It is not a den of fright and horrors. For almost all of human existence, it has been home, and the wild animals have been our neighbors.

Right now worldwide, more than five hundred thousand people die each year in road accidents. Two-thirds of these deaths involve pedestrians, of whom one-third are children. Just in the United States about forty six thousand people die per year because of auto collisions. About thirty thousand Americans die each year from respiratory illness stemming from auto-related airborne toxins. Yet I am not afraid of cars. Perhaps I should be. One hundred thousand Americans die every year from toxins and other workplace hazards. Around the world, two million people per year are killed through direct violence by other people. Almost five million people die each year from smoking. And how many people do bears kill? About one every other year in all of North America.

We are afraid of the wrong things.

As I write these words, two gray jays hop back and forth from the soft tips of redwood branches to the slender stems of huckleberries growing outside my window. The birds are too big for the stems to hold, so they flutter their wings to maintain balance while they stab at the by-now shriveled berries. The fluttering only works for so long, and quickly they hop back to the nearby branches. They swallow, and back they go to the huckleberries.

WHEN WAS THE LAST TIME you asked a wild nonhuman how he or she was doing? When was the last time you even considered what life might be like for one of these others? When was the last time you cared? It can be easy for us to forget, surrounded as we are by concrete and steeped in work and other activities, that the real world still exists, and it is inhabited by real beings.

I hate the sounds of chainsaws, automobiles, and heavy machinery. Can you imagine how much more these others must hate these sounds? How much would I hate and fear the sound of chainsaws if I knew they were used to tear apart my home?

This is why I leave out food for bears.

Wood rats sometimes move from the forest into my mom's garage. I catch them in live-traps and take them back where they came from to maintain the prey base for the spotted owls I sometimes hear calling back and forth through the trees. I leave food for slugs because they were here before me and also because I share this land with red-legged frogs, who are elsewhere declining and for whom slugs are a primary food. Helping the slugs helps the slugs, and it helps the frogs, it helps the pacific giant salamanders, it helps the snakes, and it helps my other neighbors.

If wild animals were not everywhere being terrified and tormented, having their food sources taken away and their homes destroyed, being forced to adapt to increasingly hostile and antibiotic conditions, and being increasingly subjected to what can only be labeled a final solution, I would still offer them food as a sign of respect and neighborliness. Because they are being systematically exterminated, however, I feed and help them how I can as a sign of resistance and solidarity. Had I been alive in the early nineteenth century, I would have done the same for the humans on the Underground Railroad. In Nazi Germany, I would have done the same for Jews, homosexuals, Romani, communists, anarchists, Jehovah's Witnesses, members of the resistance, and others.

We all need sanctuaries. The degree to which I can use whatever skills I possess to provide them for those who are being exploited is the degree to which I can be proud and happy to be who I am.

In today's *San Francisco Chronicle* there is a full-page ad for the zoo's grizzly bear exhibit put out by the zoo that begins, "It is a story both heartwarming and bittersweet. The two grizzly bears that [sic] will be welcomed by the public this weekend at the San Francisco Zoo were wild-born animals whose misfortune [sic] has turned into a second chance at life." The ad maintains this tone throughout, later saying, "Orphaned at a young age [how, the ad does not say], the pair nevertheless survived, and through ingenuity—or perhaps just convenience of food sources—a hapless rancher's grain storage area became the bears' bread and butter. But bears and humans don't exactly mix well, and the bears were suddenly down to their last strike, as this was not the first time they had invaded territory not their own." Yes, you read all that correctly.

There are some interesting points to note about this ad. First, it exaggerates the actual damage: "bread and butter" makes it sound like the "hapless" rancher was the sole source of food for the grizzlies, but 150 pounds of corn split between two growing bears doesn't constitute a mainstay. The ad wouldn't be quite so effective with copy like, "These bears were taken from the wild because they ate about twenty dollars worth of corn." Second, note that the use of the generic phrase "bears and humans don't mix well" makes it sound as though bears cause as many problems for humans as humans do for bears. The statement is wrong anyway; humans and bears lived together on this continent for thousands of years prior to the arrival of civilization. It would be more accurate to say that life and civilization don't mix well, and more accurate still to say that civilization destroys life. The third and probably most important point to note is the classic trick used by exploiters everywhere: the ad reverses victim and exploiter. The bears are not the victims—even though they were captured and imprisoned, and are now being used for entertainment in a city and as a draw to raise attendance (read, money) at a zoo, and more broadly are victims of a way of life that leads humans to perceive nonhumans as being unworthy of consideration as in-dividuals—instead, the real victim to be pitied is the "hapless" rancher who lost so much corn. The real exploiters are the bears, who "invaded" territory that was "not their own."

Most interesting, however, is the bottom third of the ad, a "Grizzly Bear Naming Contest Entry Form" that reads, "You can help us name the San Francisco Zoo's new grizzly bears! There are two female bears, one is blonde, the other chocolate-colored. Please submit a name for each of them. Names should be Native American origin. You can find names on the Internet or via your local library." And in the largest letters of all: "Win a Grizzly Bear Prize Basket!"[33]

Bears are not toys. They are not symbols or stand-ins for Native American cultures. They are not attractions. They are not tourist destinations. They are not sources of revenue. They are not resources to be managed. They are not pests to be exterminated.

They are bears.

No, even that isn't right. There is this bear, with needs, desires, and preferences all her own. And there is that bear, whose needs, desires, and preferences will certainly overlap with another bear's but will not be identical, because the bears are not identical. Every bear—every animal, inside or outside of zoos—is an individual. Each one has, believe it or not, a life.

I'M AT A ZOO. I'm horrified. All across the zoo I see consoles atop small stands. Each console has a cartoony design clearly aimed at children, and each has a speaker with a button. When I push the button I hear a voice begin the singsong, *All the animals in the zoo are eagerly awaiting you.* The song ends by reminding the children to be sure and "get in on the fun."

I push the button. I hear the song. I look at the concrete walls, the glassed-in spaces, the moats, the electrified fences. I see the expressions on the animals' faces, so different from the expressions of the many wild animals I've seen. And I have seen the similarities between the eyes of imprisoned humans and the eyes of those imprisoned in zoos. If you will only care to look, you will see the differences, and you will see the similarities.

Again I push the button: *All the animals in the zoo are eagerly awaiting you.* The central conceit of the zoo, and in fact the central conceit of this whole culture, is that all these others have been placed here for us, that they do not have any existence independent of us, that the fish in the oceans are waiting there for us to catch them, that the trees in the forests are waiting there for us to cut them down, that the animals in the zoo are waiting there for us to be entertained by them.

It may be flattering in an infantile sort of way to believe that everything is here to serve you, but in the real world where real creatures exist and real creatures suffer, it's pretty pathetic to pretend nobody matters but you.

Not only journalists and copywriters are narcissists. Unfortunately we live in an entire culture suffering from narcissism, or to be more precise, we live in an entire world suffering from this culture's narcissism. Zoo proponents are especially prone to narcissism; they have to be or they couldn't rationalize zoos. In the book *Zoo Culture: The Book About Watching People Watch Animals,* Bob Mullan and Garry Marvin ask, "Why preserve wildlife at all? One might well respond that the world would be impoverished if the animals under threat of extinction were allowed [sic] to die out. But who precisely would be impoverished?" They then answer their own question in a way that makes this narcissism especially clear: "Our answer is that the human world would be impoverished, for animals are preserved solely for human benefit, because human beings have decided they want them to exist for human pleasure.[34] The notion that they are preserved for their sakes is a peculiar one, for it implies that animals might wish a certain condition to endure. It is, however, nonsensical for humans to imagine that animals might want to continue the existence of their species." It is obvious that neither of these authors has ever known any real wild animals, and certainly has never bothered to ask — either literally or metaphorically—these animals whether they want to survive. Of course an utter disinterest in the perspective of the other is one of the defining characteristics of narcissism.[35] Far worse than a disinterest, however, is this denial that the other's perspective even exists.

Contrast their words with those of Bill Frank Jr., Chair of the Northwest Indian Fisheries Commission, who stated, "If the salmon could speak, he would ask us to help him survive. This is something we must tackle together."[36] And I would say that the salmon are already speaking, if only we would listen. Mullan and Marvin continue, "Animals other than man [sic] cannot have a sense of species identity; they cannot reflect on the nature of their collective identity; nor can they have a sense that it would be a good thing for them to continue in existence." The authors' assertions are unsupportable, arrogant, and absolutely necessary to justify the continuation of the extermination of nonhumans. Again they continue, "The desire for a species to continue is merely a projection on the part of human beings." Once again unsupported, unsupportable, and necessary. Again: "The preservation of the natural world is only a preservation for our benefit."[37]

The authors also argue against giving zoo animals larger cages, saying that because animals generally stay in one part of the cage, they don't need a larger territory. They cite another zoo proponent's quip that cheetahs stay in only one part of their cage because "unlike Jogging Man, they saw no point in needlessly expending all that energy." Mullan and Marvin add, "The desire for space, in other words, is the public's desire, not the animals'. According to Dick van Dam, of Blijdorp Zoo, Rotterdam, 'The animals don't need the space but the public of course wants to see them roam on the big plain.'"[38] Professor H. Hediger of the Zurich Zoo expands on these same ideas: "The cage used to be something in which a wild animal was incarcerated against its will, chiefly to prevent its escape. Wild animals lived in cages like convicts in prison. This led to the idea, largely extinct today but still smouldering among some people with little knowledge of animals, that animals in the zoo were indeed convicts and innocent convicts at that, pining away in grief, sorrow, and resentment at the loss of their 'golden freedom' and frequently dying of homesickness." Hediger is saying that if we believe that animals feel—and remember, humans are animals, too—then we must have "little knowledge of animals." He continues, "Today the idea that zoo animals are in any way like innocent convicts is just as fanciful as the belief that the voices in the radio emanate from little men imprisoned in the box." Now if we believe animals feel—and remember, humans are animals, too—then according to Dr. Hediger, we must be crazy. He keeps going: "Wild animals in the zoo rather resemble estate owners. Far from desiring to escape and regain their freedom, they are only bent on defending the space they inhabit and on keeping it safe from intrusion."[39] Need I comment on this, or is it as obvious to you as it is to me that this way of thinking is insane? Time and again we see the same rationale with slightly different words. Here are the words of yet another zookeeper: "If you had to spend a weekend in a superdome without contact with other people, you would be going up the wall with boredom by Monday morning. But if I locked you in this office (a small one) for the weekend, and gave you a radio, books, pencils and so forth, you would keep yourself occupied."[40]

I'm sure you can see the fallacies. First, these animals are not locked in these cages only over a weekend, but for their lives. Second, the options are not solely whether the animals should be locked in a small cage or a large one—an office or a superdome. The zookeeper ignores the third option: to blow up both the office and the superdome, the small cage and the large one, and let the animals go. Or even better: to not capture the animals in the first place. Next, if the animals need only a small space and do not wish to roam—or, as Hediger put it, the animals have ceased "desiring to escape and regain their freedom"—then surely there would be no need for bars, moats, or electrified fences. Again, I can tell that none of these zookeepers has ever had a meaningful relationship with—or, for that matter, even truly seen—any wild animal. Have they never seen sea lions surfing, or seagulls playing in the wind? Haven't they seen wolfpacks playing together, and deer prancing and playing from joy? Have they never seen squirrels racing up and down trees, teasing each other and teasing dogs and others who cannot climb to catch them? I used to raise chickens, and on cold nights I would bring the motherless chicks inside. Each morning when I'd

take them back into the sun they would leap and dance and turn pirouettes. They would play. Both wild and domestic animals—and this is the birthright of all of us, including humans, though civilized humans have been forced to forget this—spend a tremendous amount of time playing. It's a lot of what we do. It's a lot of why we're here.

I FINISHED WRITING THIS LAST PARAGRAPH a couple of hours ago, then went out under the stars—how many zoo animals never again get to see the stars or the moon at night?—and then I came back inside. Throughout that time I thought about those cheetahs staying in one part of their cage. Then I thought about the writers of those pro-zoo books. I'll bet the writers spend a lot of time in their offices, sitting in front of their computers, writing books and articles and reading email. Like so many others in this culture, they might spend a lot of time sitting in front of a television, or maybe sitting on a couch listening to music, talking to friends. But just because they spend the majority of their time sitting in one place doesn't mean they'd want iron bars to drop down and trap them there. I wish I could imprison the people who write those books, imprison zookeepers to give them a taste of their own medicine. I would confine them for a week, for two weeks, for three weeks, and then ask them if they're still eager to make jokes about "Jogging Man" and snide comments about the loss of their "golden freedom." I would ask them if they feel grief, sorrow, resentment, and homesickness, and ask them if they still believe that animals do not need space, if they still believe that animals do not need freedom. I wouldn't listen to their answers, because I would not care to hear about their experiences. In fact, I wouldn't believe that these zookeeper animals—for humans are animals, too—meaningfully experience the world, which means it would be a projection on my part to believe they have anything to tell me. Indeed, it would be a projection on my part to believe these animals—for humans are animals, too—might wish a certain condition to continue or change. It would be a mistake to believe they even wish to continue to exist, or—and I'm thinking about monkeys and rats and other animals in laboratories—that they may wish not to be tortured. I would leave the human animals there, in their cages, and I would ask them these questions again in a year, and in five years, and in twenty-five years. During that time they would never be allowed to speak to another human, but they would be given cardboard boxes and paper bags to play with. I think that after five years they would tell me that they agreed that animals need freedom. And I would not listen to them. I would not hear them. I think that in ten years they would tell me again that animals need freedom. And I would not listen to them. I would not hear them. I would not believe they could speak. I think that in twenty-five years they would no longer tell me anything at all, but they would probably walk around their cages—their HABITATS™—taking seven steps forward, dipping their heads, turning to the left, and so on.

ACCORDING TO AN ARTICLE from the *San Diego Union-Tribune,* the incessant pacing and head dipping of imprisoned animals is not a sign of insanity. In the words of a zoo "educator," the animal performs these behaviors "because it's relaxing." The zoo's chief animal behaviorist stated, "I don't think that it's bad. It may be that it's just part of their natural behavior and we just don't fully understand that yet." The article continues, "Animal behaviorists have many theories why the bears are pacing. Some believe certain animals may be genetically predisposed to pace, while others have suggested that polar bears in the wild go into a state of 'walking hibernation' while traveling long distances, which could explain the urge to pace in the cage." Another theory: "Zoo officials also acknowledged that the cubs could be pacing 'because they feel unsettled after undergoing several moves since they were rescued from the wild.'"[41] Or maybe they pace because the bears have been driven insane by boredom, homesickness, and claustrophobia—but neither the journalist nor the zookeepers can bring themselves to mention that possibility.

At least the bears have the excuse of a lifetime of captivity and boredom to explain away their insanity.

When I wrote that many zookeepers and pro-zoo authors have clearly never had a relationship with or even really seen wild animals, I didn't mean to say that they have never interacted with wild animals. I'm reasonably certain that many probably interact on some level with wild animals on a routine basis. But mere interaction does not automatically imply relationship, nor does it imply really seeing the other. If your interactions are exploitative or otherwise require imbalances of power between the parties and lead to an increase in these imbalances, then of course increased interactions increasingly eliminate any possibility for relationship as well as the possibility of really seeing the other.

Zookeepers aren't the only ones who interact exploitatively with their surroundings. Deforesters routinely interact with forests. Many claim to love forests, even as they exploit and destroy them. Vivisectors routinely interact with animals (though they generally have the honesty to not claim they love those they exploit). SS guards routinely interacted with concentration camp inmates (and many of the Nazi doctors did everything they could to alleviate inmate suffering so long as they never questioned keeping the inmates behind electrified fences). Pornographers and pimps routinely interact with women. Many claim to love women, even as they exploit them. Interacting with women does not imply knowing them. It does not even imply seeing them for who they are.

What George Draffan and I wrote about science and surveillance in our book *Welcome to the Machine* applies equally to zoos: "Surveillance, and this is true for science [and zoos] as well—indeed, this is true for the entire culture, of which surveillance and science [and zoos] are just holographic parts—is based on unequal relationships. Surveillance—and science [and a zoo]—requires a watcher and a watched, a controller and a controlled, one who has the right to surveil or observe—with knowledge, truth, providence, and most of all, might on his side—and one who is there for the other to gain [entertainment from, or] knowledge—as power—about.

"These unequal relationships—of watcher, watched, controller, controlled—require a split, a separation. There can be no real mixing of categories, of participants. The lines between watcher and watched, controller and controlled, must be sharp and inviolable. Humans on one side, non-humans on the other. Men on one side, women on the other. Those in power on one side, the rest of us on the other. Guards on one side, prisoners on the other…." If this sounds a lot like the pornographic relationship, that's because it is. Pornography—cousin to surveillance, and bastard child of science—requires the same dynamic of watcher and watched, the same dyad of unchanged subject gazing at object to be explored at an emotional distance, the same relationship of powerful viewer looking at powerless object."[42]

And so do zoos.

As Mullan and Marvin say, in a line of theirs I finally agree with, "Zoos represent the power of human beings to command the presence of living creatures which [sic] would normally absent themselves from human gaze."[43]

I go to a zoo. I see animals on display. I push a button and hear: *All the animals in the zoo are eagerly awaiting you.*

I come home. I open a newspaper and see an article titled, "Animal Planet: From India's famed camel fair to Indonesia's fierce Komodo dragons—all the world's a zoo." And the subhead, large font, boldface: **"Animal World Awaits."**[44] For whom? For you, of course.

I put down the newspaper and turn on the computer. I go to a porn site. I see women on display. I click a mouse and read, "All my ladies love to undress in front of the camera and have a great time doing all the photo sessions that you get to view totally uncensored." I click again and read, "These girls are *sex crazy, they can't get enough!*" Again, "Hi guys, I'm Pamela! I just started my freshman year at college. Recently I shot my first uncensored hardcore fuck video and want YOU to see me fucked in all holes. I hope that you come inside to see me soon:" And again: "Cock it, load it, shoot it inside her. She's got the proper lubrication and she wants to be your target. Unload your big guns all over Christy. There's a battle brewing between her thighs, and she's waiting for you to come extinguish the flames. In the heat of the moment, when her body is raging with desire, she waits for the cavalry. Her body is a battlefield. You are her last hope. Unleash your big guns deep inside. Fill her up with all you got."

It's not enough to put these others on display. We must convince ourselves that they are desperately willing participants in their own degradation, that we are not exploiting them but doing them a favor. We are rescuing bears from the wild, saving orphans from sentences of death. The animals in zoos are so happy that we need cages to keep the others out. The animals are rich, estate owners leading lives of idle luxury. I click the computer mouse and read, "There are now reported to be one dozen Gorillas and one dozen Chimpanzees living in this new slice of Ape heaven. *They all want to meet you.*"

I push a button. I hear, *All the animals in the zoo are eagerly awaiting you.*

THIS CULTURE IS KILLING THE PLANET. In part this is because of how we perceive the world. We act according to the way we experience the world. We experience the world according to how we perceive it. We perceive it the way we have been taught. If we are to have any chance of survival, we need to change how we perceive the world.

A Canadian lumberman once said: "When I look at trees I see dollar bills." If when you look at trees you see dollar bills you will act a certain way. If when you look at trees you see trees you will act a different way. If when you look at this tree right here you see this tree right here, you will act differently still. If when you look at women you see orifices you will act a certain way. If when you look at women you see women you will act a different way. If when you look at this woman right here you see this woman right here, you will act differently still.

How do zoos teach us to perceive nonhuman animals and our relationship to them?

Maybe we can get part of the answer from a front page article in the *San Francisco Chronicle* entitled "Grizzlies turn into cash cows." The subtitle tells the story: "Free public contest is dumped in favor of getting big bucks from highest bidder—corporate or individual." In the end, the zoo's "contest" to name the newly imprisoned grizzlies was—and why should this surprise us?—little more than a public relations campaign. At the same time the zoo was ceaselessly promoting this "contest" through all available media, saying "People like the idea of naming them. It gives them a special bond," it was also "courting donors and preparing for an April 29 naming auction at ZooFest, an annual fund-raising gala." The zoo hopes to raise $30,000.[45]

As zoos demonstrate, within this culture everything is for sale. Recently a new species of monkey was "discovered" in South America. The person who "discovered" the species auctioned off the naming rights. A casino paid $650,000 to name the primate GoldenPalace.com Monkey.

I'm not making this up. I couldn't if I tried.

Again, what is the point of zoos? What do they teach us about our relationship to nonhuman animals?

Today the *San Francisco Chronicle* carried an article entitled "Shark hits 100th day at grateful aquarium: Great White adds to survival record—and to gross receipts."

Great white sharks generally do not survive captivity. Prior to this fish the record was sixteen days. And now? As the article states, "Every day that she fails to go belly up, the nameless shark sets a record for longevity in captivity. This makes the Monterey Bay Aquarium a very happy place." Why? "Ticket sales [at $20 per person] have doubled, shark merchandise sells swimmingly, 'great white' wine has been added to the restaurant menu, an entire gift store has been converted from selling jellyfish trinkets to shark trinkets, and the children's craft center is churning out 200 crayon-decorated paper shark hats a day."

The article lists some of the merchandise available in the gift shop: "$15 shark boxer shorts, $70 neon shark lamps, $3 shark bottle openers, $35 shark silk scarves, $70 shark puppets, $13 shark thermal coffee mugs, and a dozen models of plush toy sharks, each more cuddly than the last."

It concludes with a quote from a store clerk, "We don't sell that much jellyfish stuff anymore. It's all sharks, sharks, sharks."[46]

This is the essence of the spectacle: absent relationship, emotionally benumbed, ever-increasing novelty is required to maintain a sense of "feeling," a sense of "excitement." This is the essence of zoos. One former assistant director of the National Zoological Park wrote, in a book entitled, significantly enough, *The World's a Zoo*, "One reason we have so many species is that zoo men, like museum curators, are enthusiastic collectors. If a zoo director has never had [sic] kiwis, lesser pandas, colobus monkeys, Chinese alligators, marbled cats, or Komodo monitors, he wants them. A curator of reptiles wants almost any species he has never had before, the rarer the better. In zoo circles, it is a mark of distinction to have what no one else has. A collection of common species may please the public, but it is the rare items that [sic] make for status in the zoo community."[47]

The thrill is purely in the novelty, as with a rare stamp or coin. It isn't in the animals themselves, who are in this purview nothing more nor less than commodities.

Portfolio One

CONTAINED

African lion, *Panthera leo:* East and southern Africa

Pygmy hippopotami, *Hexaprotodon liberiensis*, West Africa

Siberian tigers (Amur tiger), *Panthera tigris altaica:* Amur-Ussuri region of eastern Russia, Manchuria, North Korea

Western lowland gorillas *Gorilla gorilla gorilla:* Angola, Cameroon, Central African Republic, Democratic Republic of the Congo, Gabon, Republic of Equitorial Guinea

Sun bear, *Helarctos malayanus:* Southeast Asia

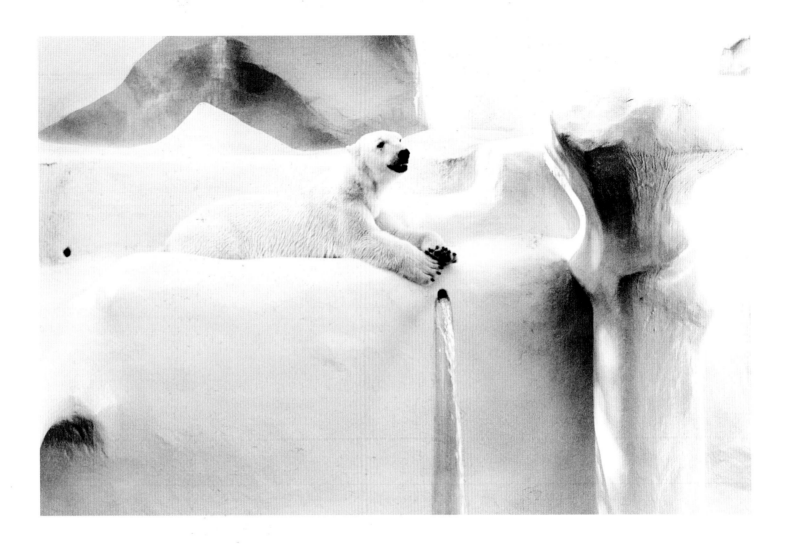

Polar bear, *Ursus maritimus*: Arctic regions of Alaska, Canada, Greenland, Norway, Russia

Polar bear, *Ursus maritimus:* Arctic regions of Alaska, Canada, Greenland, Norway, Russia

Western lowland gorillas, *Gorilla gorilla gorilla:* Angola, Cameroon, Central African Republic, Democratic Republic of the Congo, Gabon, Republic of Equitorial Guinea

Black rhinoceros, *Diceros bicornis:* East, West, and South-central Africa

Sumatran tiger, *Panthera tigris sumatrae*: Sumatra

African lions, *Panthera leo:* East and southern Africa

White rhinoceros, *Ceratotherium simum:* Northeastern and southern Africa

Reticulated giraffe, *Giraffa camelopardalis reticulata*: Ethiopia, Kenya, Somalia

Grévy's zebras, *Equus grevyi*: Eastern Africa

Puma (cougar, mountain lion), *Puma concolor*: North and South America

North American bison, *Bison bison:* Small continuously wild populations
remain in Yellowstone National Park and Alberta, Canada

Orangutan, *Pongo ponginae:* Islands of Borneo and Sumatra

Asian elephant, *Elephas maximus:* Bangladesh, Cambodia, southern China, India,
Indonesia, Laos, Malaysia, Myanmar, Nepal, Sri Lanka, Thailand, Vietnam

Mandrills, *Mandrillus sphinx:* Cameroon, Democratic Republic of the Congo, Gabon, Republic of Equitorial Guinea

Celebes crested macaque (Celebes monkey, Sulawesi crested macaque, black ape),
Macaca nigra: Sulawesi, Indonesia and other small neighboring islands Cameroon,
Democratic Republic of the Congo, Gabon, Republic of Equitorial Guinea

Asian elephant, *Elephas maximus*: Bangladesh, Cambodia, southern China, India, Indonesia, Laos, Malaysia, Myanmar, Nepal, Sri Lanka, Thailand, Vietnam

IT IS OFTEN SAID that one of the primary positive functions of zoos is education. The standard ending to the standard zoo book uses high blown language to state that because the earth has become a battle-field, with the animals losing the battle and the war, that zoos really are the last hope for beleaguered wildlife. Only through unleashing the full potential of zoos for education will the mass of people ever grow to care enough about wildlife to not destroy the planet. The challenge of zoos, according to one not atypical passage, is, "To allow living, breathing animals to inspire wonder and awe of the natural world; to teach us that animal's place in the cosmos and to illuminate the tangled and fragile web of life that sustains it; to open the door to conservation for the millions of people who want to help save this planet and the incredible creatures it contains. To enrich, enlighten and empower the people who care, so that through huge numbers and sheer willpower we save the beetle and the snail and the alligator along with the panda and the rhino and the condor."[48]

Let's parse this out. The author Vicki Croke's use of the word "allow" carries with it the same old implication of will-ingness on the part of the encaged, ignoring that they are forcibly imprisoned: and saying that we must capture and imprison these others so we can then allow them to teach us. Her word *allow* would be entirely appropriate if we were talking about wild animals in wild circumstances coming to us as educators. Within many indigenous cosmologies wild creatures are our primary teachers. I think often of the words of Brave Buffalo, "I have noticed in my life that all men have a liking for some special animal, tree, plant, or

spot of earth. If men would pay more attention to these preferences and seek what is best to do in order to make themselves worthy of that toward which they are attracted, they might have dreams which would purify their lives. Let a man decide upon his favorite animal and make a study of it, learning its innocent ways. Let him learn to understand its sounds and motions. The animals want to communicate with man, but Wakan'tanka [the Great Spirit] does not intend they shall do so directly—man must do the greater part in securing an understanding."[49]

And what, according to Vicki Croke, will these incarcer-ated animals—oh, sorry, these estate owners—teach us? They will "inspire wonder and awe of the natural world."

Have you ever been to a zoo? Zoos consist of row after row, promenade after promenade, of animals in cages—oh, sorry, habitats. Zoos are at their very best weak simulations of the natural world. So what can at best be conveyed is a sense of appreciation for the cleverness of those who attempt these simulations as well as befuddlement that anyone would even try (why try—and fail miserably—to replicate nature when nature does it for free?).

And have you seen the people at zoos? The pacing grizzly bear did not elicit any response at all from those who passed by, much less wonder and awe. And what feelings are inspired by the hippopotamus drifting in a concrete tank of turds and water; the chained elephant; the lonely giraffe? Awe and wonder would be entirely inappropriate, unless they are at the resilience of these creatures in the face of these horrors. Zoos do not inspire a sense of awe and wonder in me. They inspire a sense of loneliness and deep sorrow.

I see no awe and wonder on the faces of other zoo patrons. I hear children laughing at the animals. Not the sweet sound of children's laughter that we so often read about in bad poems, but the derisive laughter of the school-yard, the laughter at someone else's misfortunes, the laughter that gives voice to the same contempt manifested in flippant newspaper headlines and in "Jogging Man" jokes. I see moth-ers with their young children, laughing with the children, pointing at the silly animals, laughing at the fat orangutan, laughing at the pacing wolf, making scary faces at the snake, ignoring the pacing bear, laughing at the anteater walking back and forth, back and forth, endlessly back and forth. And the women with their strollers, with their young children crying for cotton candy, crying for plush bears, never stop walking, never stop talking, never stop pointing and laughing. They enter the monkey house. They shriek at the silly monkeys, the silly chimpanzees who pick their noses and who stare straight through the glass at the women, at the children. The children laugh and pound on the glass. They put their faces close to it, stare back at the animal on the other side. Make faces. I turn away. I hear the mothers shriek again, say, "Oh, look, the monkey is doing a poopie." I close my eyes, find myself again gripping a rail. The children laugh and scream. The mothers shriek yet one more time, and say, "Oh, look, the monkey is smearing his poopie on the glass." The women and children laugh and laugh.

I think, "Don't you know what that chimpanzee just said to you? Are you so insensate you do not even know when you've been insulted?" What are these women and children learning? What "awe and wonder" are they "allowing" the animals to inspire?

Croke continues that a purpose of zoos is "to teach us that animal's place in the cosmos and to illuminate the tangled and fragile web of life that sustains it." This makes no sense. Zoos teach us that a hippo's place is in a turd-filled concrete pool, a monkey's place is behind glass so he can't smear shit on our faces—which at this point he would surely love to do—and a grizzly's place is in a ten thousand square foot "habitat." How could a zoo teach us an animal's place in the cosmos when the creature's presence in the zoo requires the creature or his or her ancestors to have been forcibly removed from that rightful place? And how could a zoo illuminate a tangled and fragile web when all of the component parts are split apart and caged? The web consists of the relationships between the different animals and plants and soils and weather and cannot be simulated in a concrete box, no matter how much "enrichment" is added.

Vicki Croke has a lot of company. David Hancocks uses similarly self-congradulatory language to once again convey the notion that zoos are nature's last hope: "Zoos have the marvelous potential to develop a concerned, aware, energized, enthusiastic, caring, and sympathetic citizenry. Zoos can encourage gentleness toward all other animals and compassion for the well-being of wild places. Zoos can cultivate environmental sensitivity among their hundreds of millions of patrons. Such a populace might then want to live more lightly on the land, be more careful about using the world's natural resources, and actually choose to vote for politicians who care about the wild inhabitants of the Earth and the health of the wild places that remain. To help save all wildlife, to work toward a healthier planet, to encourage a more sensitive populace: these are the goals for the new zoos."[50]

We could parse this out the same as we did for Vicki Croke to find the same unfounded assumptions and magical thinking, but it might be better if you just go to a zoo for yourself and watch the patrons.

Even if we accept their claims for the educational potential of zoos at face value, study after study has shown that zoos fail miserably at this task. As one author notes, "A study of observation periods at Regent's Park in 1985 revealed that spectators stood in front of the monkey enclosure for an average of 46 seconds, and spent 32 minutes in a pavilion containing a hundred cages. Rather than indicating thorough examination, this is reminiscent of the speed at which television programmes, and even works of art in museums, are 'consumed.'"[51] This 46 seconds includes time spent reading—or rather skimming—the information posted about the animals. Further, while 80 percent of zoo visitors claim to have learned something at the zoo, studies have shown that even after their visit patrons remain "less sensitive to the need to respect nature" than hikers.[52] Further still, inquiry after inquiry has revealed that even while patrons are in the zoo, standing directly in front of the animals in question, they consistently fail even rudimentary nomenclature questions: they still call gibbons and orangutans *monkeys;* vultures *buzzards;* cassowaries *peacocks;* toucans *fruitloop birds;* tigers *lions;* otters *beavers;* and so on.

Peter Batten comments on the educational value of zoos: "Whether anyone derives lasting benefit by seeing wild animals from other countries in enclosures which inhibit their natural behavior must be evaluated without bias. Should one learn that the chimpanzee, for example, is a neurotic humanoid that cadges food from humans, and throws tantrums and excreta should this not materialize? Or that the orangutan, which [who] by nature seldom descends to the soft forest floor, is a pathetic bundle of matted red fur in the corner of a tiled cell? Must the alert, gregarious California sea lion be represented by an animal, half blinded from filthy unsalted water, that [who] spends its life begging for rotten fish?"[53]

All this said, I actually think zoos overwhelmingly succeed at teaching visitors about nonhumans. But the question remains: what are they teaching?

I have before me a photograph from a book written by zookeeper and pro-zoo philosopher David Hancocks. The photo shows a primate reaching one hand through steel bars. The caption's start tells us almost everything we need to know about the real lessons taught at zoos: "A Celebes macaque stretches an arm forlornly to the world outside its [sic] sterile cage at the Paignton Zoo, England. It would be easy to misinterpret this as a mute appeal for help and consolation from its enforced isolation...."[54] The real lesson of zoos is that we should never trust our empathic response to the suffering of these others.

THE NUMBER OF ZOOS in Europe crashed with the decline and fall of the Roman Empire. Zoos require not only an urban population deprived of daily contact with large wild animals but also an empire to provide a steady supply of fresh animals to replace those who die in captivity. In addition, systematic hunting had depopulated large swaths of North Africa and the Middle East, making exotic animals a luxury fewer rulers could afford.

Zoos did not disappear entirely from Europe. They remained in the courts of kings and emperors, like Charlemagne, who maintained a menagerie, and in the Byzantine Empire: the remnants of the eastern half of the Roman Empire. Crusaders returning from the region seem to have brought the idea of zoos back with them, at first to Italy and then to the rest of Europe. Soon the increasing wealth of those in power led to something of a prestige race, with nobles attempting to consolidate or improve their reputations through exclusive pastimes and conspicuous consumption. This included owning wild animals. Local animals were sometimes owned, but, in the words of Eric Baratay and Elisabeth Hardouin-Fugier in their stunning *Zoo: A History of Zoological Gardens in the West,* "exotic animals were much sought after since they reinforced the impression of their owners' power, particularly when ferocious and shown in pairs."[55]

There was an explosion in the number of zoos in Europe with the start of the Age of Empire, sometimes misnamed the Age of Discovery, as European empires expanded across the globe. Wild animals flooded into Europe along with human slaves, gold, and other commodities. John Berger pointed out, "When they were founded—the London Zoo in 1828, the Jardin des Plantes in 1793, the Berlin Zoo in 1844—they brought considerable prestige to the national capitals. The prestige was not so different from that which had accrued to the private royal menageries. These menageries, along with gold plate, architecture, orchestras, players, furnishings, dwarfs, acrobats, uniforms, horses, art and food, had been demonstrations of an emperor's or king's power and wealth. Likewise in the 19th century, public zoos were an endorsement of modern colonial power. The capturing of the animals was a symbolic representation of the conquest of all distant and exotic lands. Explorers proved their patriotism by sending home a tiger or an elephant. The gift of an exotic animal to the metropolitan zoo became a token in subservient diplomatic relations."[56] Berger is not the only one to make this point. It was commonly accepted at the time, and it is commonly accepted today, that the zoos of the nineteenth century, as another writer puts it, "symbolized its [the zoo's] owner's triumph over the natural world," and that "the zoo became a symbol of colonial conquest as well as of wealth and status."[57]

We could modify David Hancocks's inaccurate statement again, and say, "Zoos have evolved independently in all empires around the globe." Zoos are symbols of empire.

Zoos are about power.

45

But you knew that already, didn't you?

While it's true that, as Berger wrote, "The capturing of animals was a symbolic representation of the conquest of all distant and exotic lands," and it is true that zoos are symbols of wealth and power, we must never forget that there is much more at stake here than mere symbols, especially to those most intimately involved.

In the age of the Roman Empire, pits and traps were traditionally favored for capturing most animals. Injuries were common, often fatal. Even animals not physically injured did not emerge unscathed. In addition to forever losing their freedom, obviously, Baratay and Hardouin-Fugier report, "The shock of being captured was such that, according to tamers, 'a big cat [would] be almost mad upon arrival.'"[58] Historically, about 50 percent of animals died on ships bound for Europe or America. Baratay and Hardouin-Fugier write that "Deaths before embarkation cannot even be guessed at. For most monkeys and for some other animals, the destruction of mothers and, effectively, of their descendants must also be counted. James Fisher, an assistant manager of London Zoo, estimated that one captured orang-utan eliminates four in the wild, of whom three would be potential mothers. Domalain reckoned the number of animals killed for every one visible at a zoo to be ten. Even in the twentieth century, mortality rates for legitimate air transport continued to be high: between 1988 and 1991, they were between 10 and 37 percent for baboons and long-tailed monkeys from Africa, around 10 percent from the Philippines, and 18–54 percent from Indonesia."[59]

The traditional method for capturing many social creatures, including elephants, gorillas, chimpanzees, and many others, was—and remains—to kill the mothers. About elephants it was said, "The only way to capture a living animal was to kill the suckling females or the herd's leaders. The account of the Tornblad expedition to Kenya tells of the slaughter of adult giraffes that enabled the capture of a calf, who was immediately welcomed into the group, cared for and given a name, Rosalie. Hagenbeck found himself 'too often obliged to kill' elephants who were protecting their young by using their own bodies as shields."[60]

Just keep telling yourself: they're only animals. They don't feel. They don't care. They don't grieve. The mothers and fathers do not love their children. The children do not love their parents. Keep repeating that it is a peculiar notion to believe that animals might wish a certain condition to endure.

I think it best to describe the capture of zoo animals in the words of those humans most directly involved. I cannot improve on their language.

Hans Dominik was a German living in Africa around the start of the twentieth century. He extensively captured and traded many types of animals, including human animals. Here he describes capturing elephants for transport to zoos. "There was little activity among the animals. The calls of the working humans which carried clearly through the quiet forest hardly appeared to bother them. One bull stood apart, preoccupied with tearing twigs off branches with his trunk and consuming the leaves. Closest to us stood a cow using her trunk to lovingly caress her baby, which was barely larger than a pig and stood between her legs. A few animals ate—sweeping together and ripping up low-growing grasses and using their trunks like sickles—most of them appeared to be sleeping…. We seemed so small, so insignificant when compared to the mighty animals in the mighty wild."[61]

How does it go? "You show power by keeping an animal captive; how much more powerful are you if you kill it?"[62]

That night Dominik and his servants built a fence to prevent the animals' escape. The "hunt" began the next morning. "One after the other, a head turning to the left to pull up something green from here and there, the elephants came slowly toward us. The safeties were released. 'You, the second,' I whispered to Zampa. Now we had the animals ready. I fired at the right ear of the foremost animal. At the sharp crack the elephant threw its trunk into the air and trumpeted loudly. The short tail stretched out far, he turned upon himself like a top. In this moment Zampa also fired. Close before me the second animal buckled at his knees, but quickly stood up again and followed the incessantly bellowing and bleeding lead bull which pushed up the hill."[63]

Dominick followed the wounded animals, continuing to fire as he went. He found them. "There lay one of the animals; apparently the spine had been hit because the elephant had only collapsed in the rear and was in a sitting position. Like columns, the forelegs projected from out of the ground, the head and trunk swung left and right: a muffled moan sounded, thick clumps of blood flowed at the side, a sign that the lungs were also wounded. The other stood next to him, motionless except for his trunk. He blew frequently, and with his trunk threw soil on himself. Our approach didn't seem to bother the animals. We crept around them. I had the eye of the sitting giant exactly in the rifle sight, when beside me Zampa fired. The standing elephant trumpeted loudly. Now I squeezed the trigger and the animal collapsed onto its side. The other elephant was still standing; finally with the first shot from my second chamber he collapsed. Close beside one another lay the two giants in a massive pool of blood. Amba and Balla were already there; with their sharp machetes they cut through the trunks, which were half the thickness of a man. The animals were still breathing. As if from a fountain, the red blood sprayed up from the thick arteries onto our clothes as we stood beside the animals examining our guns and discussed how we should proceed with the hunt."[64]

In his indispensable book *Savages and Beasts,* Nigel Rothfels details the rest of Dominik's story: "The fascination with grisly detail which permeates this story continues as the hunt progresses. Soon Dominik encountered a female with a young calf; after several shots, also graphically described, the female was dispatched with a shot in the left eye. The calf was roped to a tree, where it 'churned up the soil with its small tusks, bellowed and moaned, charged backwards, stood on its head, and foamed at the mouth in rage as bloodshot eyes protruded from its head.' Three remaining calves were soon captured as well, one dying of suffocation after having its trunk pulled between its forelegs and tied to its rear legs so that it 'breathed with difficulty and lay on the ground like a large gray sack.' Another calf died during the night of wounds sustained in the capture, but Dominik had still managed to secure two calves from the herd and soon added three more to his collection. Two died a month later, but the

remaining three apparently thrived [sic] in their new environment,[65] and one found its way through Hagenbeck to the Berlin Zoo, where it was seen by literally thousands of Berliners who lined up to view the newest acquisition from the colonies."[66]

And how does it go? *All the animals in the zoo are eagerly awaiting you.*

Heinrich Leutemann clarified the priorities of those who capture animals for zoos: "For the animal trader, the method of capture is, from a business point of view, a trivial issue."[67] He gives examples: "Without exceptions lions are captured as cubs after the mother has been killed, the same happens with tigers, because those animals, when caught as adults in such things as traps and pits, are too powerful and untamable, and usually die while resisting.... The larger anthropoid apes can, in addition, only be captured—taking into account occasional exceptions—quite young beside the killed mother. The same is the case with almost all animals; in the processes, for example, giraffes and antelopes, when hunted, simply abandon their young which have fallen behind, while in contrast the mother elephant more often defends her calf and therefore must [sic] be killed, as is the case with hippopotamuses.... Also in the case of the rhinoceros, the young are captured from the adults, which [sic] are usually killed as a result."[68]

Perhaps the most famous elephant of the nineteenth century was Jumbo. He was captured in a similar fashion. A hunter, Hermann Schomburgk, shot his mother. He describes it himself: "She collapsed in the rear and gave me the opportunity to jump quickly sideways and bring to bear a deadly shot, after which she immediately died. Obeying the laws of nature, the young animal remained standing beside its [sic] mother.... Until my men arrived, I observed how the pitiful little baby continuously ran about its mother while hitting her with his trunk as if he wanted to wake her and make their escape."[69]

MOST OF US have never heard these stories. Much better to believe that zoos rescue animals from the wild, that animals are waiting there for us, eager for us to allow them to inspire wonder and awe at the natural world.

But there is a very good reason we do not hear these

stories. To hear them too often might impinge on the fantasy that the eager beavers and ocelots and wolverines and bears and elephants and tigers are dying to meet us. Zookeepers know this. They have always known it. William Hornaday, director of the Bronx Zoo, wrote in 1902 to Carl Hagenbeck, considered by many to be the father of the modern zoological gardens and a trader in animals on an almost inconceivable scale,[70] "I have been greatly interested in the fact that your letter gives me regarding the capture of the rhinoceroses; but we must keep very still about forty large Indian rhinoceroses being killed in capturing the four young ones. If that should get into the newspapers, either here or in London, there would be things published in condemnation of the whole business of capturing wild animals for exhibition. There are now a good many cranks who are so terribly sentimental that they affect to believe that it is wrong to capture wild creatures and exhibit them—even for the benefit [sic] of millions of people. For my part, I think that while the loss of the large Indian rhinoceroses is greatly to be deplored, yet, in my opinion, the three young ones that [sic] survive will be of more benefit to the world at large than would the forty rhinoceroses running wild in the jungles of Nepal, and seen only at rare intervals by a few ignorant natives."[71]

Proponents of zoos will certainly claim that things have changed since the bad old days. As one zoo trader put it—and I quote this at length because of the grim delight he obviously takes in his work—"Who would have thought ten years ago that big game, like elephants, rhinos, hippos, and the swift gazelles and antelopes, could be captured alive by a shot from a gun? Of course, the shot consists of a hypodermic needle filled with a drug which only paralyzes the animal for a short while. The possibilities opened by this invention should be obvious to everyone. And who would have thought a few years ago that whales and dolphins could be captured, trained, used for diving tests, displayed to an interested public and sent on air journeys of many hours' duration?…[72]

"Instead of going on safari for weeks at a time with a large column of porters, the modern collector takes to the car and has a much easier time. In former days, the elephant dams had to be killed if the young was to be taken because it was impossible to get close to a herd of elephants or rhinos on foot or on horseback. Though not without risk, the car can be used to separate the mother from her offspring. Zebras, antelopes and giraffes have no chance of escape when they are pursued not only by one horse but by 100 horse power, unless they are able to reach an inaccessible area in time. The catcher stands on top of the car or sits in a seat mounted on the mudguard. He holds [a] long bamboo stick with a lassoo at its end. The other end of the lassoo is firmly secured to the car. When the car approaches the animal to be captured, the lassoo is thrown around its [sic] neck, the driver gradually reduces speed and the animal is eventually put into a container.

"Capture by lassoo from horseback was probably less harmful to the animal because a horse will tire eventually and thus give the animal a better and fairer chance to escape. On the other hand, a rider on horseback can get closer to the herd. Nowadays the noise of the engine is sufficient to make the animals run for their lives. But a car is not subject to fatigue. Unless it is skillfully done, capture by car may lead to overstrain or even complete exhaustion. Much experience, good cars, and a certain amount of imagination are essential.

"Nocturnal animals have no chance of escape when they are hunted with strong headlamps and searchlights, which dazzle their eyes so that they cannot see the hunter. For many years this method of catching the shy and swift antelopes and gazelles, and even rhinos and hippos, was strictly prohibited, but today it is in common use. When the normal headlights pick out a herd or a single animal, a strong searchlight is directed at the specimen [sic] to be captured. The hunters take advantage of its [sic] temporary blindness to put a rope around the animal, or, if it is a small animal, to catch it by hand.

"A sheer accident taught the natives of the wooded slopes of Mounts Kilimanjaro and Meru in Tanzania how to catch colobus or guereza monkeys, still relatively rarely seen in captivity. At weekends the natives would drink a home-brewed beer called pombe. It is made of Indian corn and the dregs are simply thrown away. Since guerezas very rarely climb down to the ground, the natives were amazed to see a whole colony of these monkeys climb down from the trees and crowd round the dregs, possibly attracted by the smell of alcohol. Normally they would eat only leaves but when they tried the fragrant food, they liked it and ate as much as they could. When the natives came closer, the monkeys were so drunk that they were unable to reach the trees, let alone climb them, and a large number of them had to sleep off their hangover in a European capture station."[73] Meet the new zoo, same as the old zoo.

Did I mention that zoos are about power?

Hans Dominik, enslaver of both humans and non-humans, supplier of nonhumans to zoos—it was left to others, such as Carl Hagenbeck, to supply indigenous humans to zoos, who were then displayed in cages along with the rest of the apes—believed that African elephants could be domesticated, just like their Indian cousins. About this he wrote, "In discussions of the thousands of tons of ivory which are shipped yearly from Africa and more specifically from the Congo, one hears time and again the anxious question, when will the last elephant in Africa be shot? Even if it will be a good while until then, so it would be greeted with great satisfaction, if the last wild elephant were carried to his grave by his domesticated brothers."[74]

These days zoos are minor players in the wild animal trade. Other forms of global exploitation have far surpassed them. About 80 to 90 percent of primates used in medical research, for example, are taken from the wild. The international trade in ivory has devastated elephants, and the trade in rhino horns has devastated rhinos. Many cats are endangered for their fur, and many birds, reptiles and fish are endangered for the trade in pets.

No matter the end use, the result is the same, a loss of freedom, a loss of life, a loss of contribution to the community and to the landbase.

Some animals do reproduce in zoos. This is good news for zoos, because, as Vicki Croke notes about the only thing that really matters in the world of commodities, "Baby animals attract visitors, so each zoo birth is money in the bank." But this creates another problem. Croke continues, "every birth also brings another animal to house. Often an older, less attractive member of the species must go to make room. Also, certain species become 'hot,' shoving others out of the warmth of the limelight and onto surplus lists."

These "surplus lists" are long indeed. Croke gives the numbers: "Accredited zoos and aquariums [accredited by the AAZPA, American Association of Zoological Parks and Aquariums] produce perhaps eight thousand surplus animals a year. Now, consider that accredited zoos make up only a fraction of all zoos—10 percent of the fourteen hundred licensed—and it's easy to figure that eighty thousand animals could be considered surplus each year."[75] That's just in the United States. That's more than two hundred every day, all year round.

It's hard to know exactly what happens to these "surplus" animals. For the most part zoos are not particularly forthcoming. This could be because a significant portion of these "surplus" animals—perhaps more than half—are killed. This includes healthy, young endangered animals such as Siberian tigers.

Zoos usually decide what to do with "surplus" animals based on "what the market will bear."[76] Consequently, many thousands of other "surplus" animals per year are sold to circuses, animal merchants, auctions, individual pet owners, "game farms," "hunting ranches," and "trophy collectors."[77] At least one "safari organizer" bought jaguars, leopards, and lions from zoos, then used the same plane to transport hunters and prey (in crates in the luggage compartment) to the "safari" site.[78] One of the organizer's associates described the hunt: "Sometimes the cats don't want to be free, but run back in the cage. The animals were afraid, that's why they run back into the cage. What he [the organizer] does is send the hunter to fish in the river, send the jeep with his men and they run the cat up a tree and then he'd go get the guy and let him shoot it."[79]

One businessman took the "safari" solution one step further by simultaneously directing the Fort Worth Zoo and owning the "Premier Wildlife Ranch."[80]

William Hampton, the owner of another AAZPA-accredited zoo, came up with an even more ingenious money-making scheme. For several years he bought and traded U.S. zoo animals, until a member of a local humane society discovered a fenced compound with crates bearing the names of major zoos from across the country. Peter Batten describes what happened next: "Further investigation revealed a trailer filled with the putrefying remains of dismembered animals and led to the discovery that Hampton and his associates had systematically slaughtered surplus zoo animals, skinned them, and sold heads and pelts as wall trophies. Living evidence was provided by American alligators, found with jaws taped and starving to assure unblemished hides for eventual sale."[81]

"Surplus" animals have been sold directly to taxidermists (lions, for $20 each, after ten years in another accredited zoo, where they had on one occasion been doused with gasoline and set on fire by zoo patrons just for fun).[82]

And still other "surplus" animals—many thousands of them—are vivisected, both by scientists at zoos and elsewhere. Why? As one scientist sarcastically commented, "Zoo research consists of killing animals to see what they died of."[83] The relationship between zoos and vivisection can be surmised by the fact that the Institute of Laboratory Animal Resources of the National Research Council, which exists "to promote the procurement of breeding, husbandry, and use of laboratory animals," has sponsored AAZPA meetings.

It's not just a few rogue zoos perpetrating all these atrocities. Baratay and Hardouin-Fugier summarize the results of a 1999 *San Jose Mercury News* investigation, "Many zoos and several of the 24 organizations affiliated with the AAZPA were practising illegal sales on a large scale. The studbook for giraffes… mentions six hundred animals that disappeared from view after sale (1997). The 'best zoo in the world,' San Diego, numbers among the three biggest black marketers, with a rate of 79 percent. Endangered species have not escaped the inflated market created by snobbism and speculation. The *Mercury News* conclusion: 'AAZPA-accredited zoos claim that they actively work to propose reintroduction when they purposely breed animals in order to exploit their commercial appeal and then cast them into

ignominious conditions.'"[84]

YEARS AGO I read a book whose title, author, and subject I can't remember. But the book contained one line that I'll never forget: "If animals could conceive of a devil, his image would be man's."

It's a powerful line, but I have two quibbles with it. The first is that, as I said before, not all human cultures have treated nonhumans so atrociously. Not all human cultures have enslaved them. Not all human cultures have tortured them in vivisection labs, factory farms, or elsewhere. Not all human cultures have put them in cages. Not all human cultures have driven them extinct. The reason so many of us pretend that all human cultures have done these things is because it masks the fact that these atrocities are based on choices, based on ways of experiencing the world, perceiving the world, perceiving our place in the world—or, as Vicki Croke would say, our place in the cosmos—perceiving who we are and what are our rights and responsibilities.

Everywhere there has been a civilization, animals (including human animals) have been enslaved, they have been tortured, they have been put in cages, their habitat has been destroyed, they have been driven extinct.[85] So I would change the line: If animals could conceive of a devil, his image would be civilized human's.

The second quibble I have is that I have absolutely no doubt that animals are able to conceive of a devil. So I would change it again: When animals conceive of a devil, his image is civilized human's.

If you are a mother, what would you do if someone tried to take your child? If you have a mother, what would you feel if someone shot her so they could put you on display? What would you feel as you poked at her, hit her, wanted her to wake up so together you could make your escape, but she did not awaken? What would you feel if they put you in a cage?[86]

These are not rhetorical questions. What would you do? What would you feel?

Portfolio Two

CONFINED

Eastern lowland gorilla, *Gorilla beringei graueri*: Democratic Republic of the Congo

Hamadryas baboon, *Papio hamadryas:* Egypt, Eritrea, Ethiopia, Somalia, Arabian Peninsula (population possibly introduced)

Japanese macaque (snow monkey), *Macaca fuscata*: Northern Japan

Leopard, *Panthera tigris sumatrae:*
Sub-Saharan Africa, China, India, Java, Middle East , Pakistan, Siberia, Southeast Asia, Sri Lanka

Rothschild's giraffes, *Giraffa camelopardalis rothschildi*: Kenya, Uganda

Polar bear, *Ursus maritimus:* Arctic regions of Alaska, Canada, Greenland, Norway, Russia

White-handed gibbon (Lar gibbon), *Hilobates lar*: Malay Peninsula, Sumatra, southwest China

Rothschild's giraffe, *Giraffa camelopardalis rothschildi:* Kenya, Uganda

Serval, *Leptailurus serval:* East and West Africa

Clouded leopard, *Neofelis nebulosa:* Southeast Asia, southern China,
eastern Himalayas, Indonesian archipelago, northeastern India

Rothschild's giraffe, *Giraffa camelopardalis rothschildi*: Kenya, Uganda

Slender-tailed meercat, *Suricata suricatta*: Southern Africa

Geoffroy's spider monkey (black-handed spider monkey), *Ateles geoffroyi*: Central America

Arctic fox (blue phase), *Alopex lagopus:* Circumpolar, alpine Iceland and Scandinavia

Snow leopard, *Uncia uncia or Panthera uncia*: Mountains of central Asia

Giant Pandas, *Ailuropoda melanoleuca:* China

Western lowland gorilla, *Gorilla gorilla gorilla:* Angola, Cameroon, Central African Republic, Democratic Republic of the Congo, Gabon, Republic of Equitorial Guinea

African elephant (left), *Loxodonta africana*: Sub-Saharan Africa and Asian elephant, *Elephas maximus*: Bangladesh, Cambodia, southern China, India, Indonesia, Laos, Malaysia, Myanmar, Nepal, Sri Lanka, Thailand, Vietnam

Japanese macaques (snow monkeys), *Macaca fuscata*: Northern Japan

Arabian camel (Egyptian camel, dromedary), *Camelus dromedarius*:
Extinct in its native North Africa and western Asia. Feral remnant of introduced population survives in Australia.

White Bengal tiger (color mutation of *Panthera tigris tigris*): India

Siberian tiger (Amur tiger), *Panthera tigris altaica:* Amur-Ussuri region of eastern Russia, Manchuria, North Korea

Gelada, *Theropithecus gelada*: Eritrea, Ethiopia

Rhesus macaque (Rhesus monkey), *Macaca mulatta*: Afghanistan, northern India

Western lowland gorilla, *Gorilla gorilla gorilla:* Angola, Cameroon, Central African Republic,
Democratic Republic of the Congo, Gabon, Republic of Equitorial Guinea

Giant anteater with young, *Myrmecophaga tridactyla*: Central and South America

White-handed gibbon (Lar gibbon), *Hilobates lar:* Malay Peninsula, Sumatra, southwest China

Mandrill, *Mandrillus sphinx*: Cameroon, Democratic Republic of the Congo, Gabon, Republic of Equitorial Guinea

Patas monkey, *Erythrocebus patas:* West Africa

Hippopotamus, *Hippopotamus amphibius:* Botswana, Democratic Republic of the Congo, Ethiopia, Gambia, Kenya, Mozambique, Republic of South Africa, Sudan, Tanzania, Uganda, Zambia, Zimbabwe

Mandrill, *Mandrillus sphinx*: Cameroon,
Democratic Republic of the Congo, Gabon, Republic of Equitorial Guinea

ONE OF THE THINGS I hate most about reading books and articles by zookeepers and other zoo boosters is their smugness, the self-righteousness stemming from the authors' entirely unexamined belief that humans are superior to and fundamentally different and separate from "the animals." Animals are animals and humans are not animals. An impermeable wall stands between.

Humans, they say, are intelligent. Animals—by which is meant all animals except humans—are not, or if they do have any sort of intelligence, it is dim, rudimentary, just sufficient to allow them to meaninglessly navigate their meaningless physical surroundings, just enough to allow them to be "enriched" by paper bags and cardboard boxes.[87]

Human behavior is based on conscious, rational choices (except when it comes to attempting to dominate everyone and everything around us and destroying all that is wild, in which case it must be insisted that all humans—and maybe all animals—are hardwired to dominate and destroy, meaning the massive destruction all around us—yes, that massive destruction, the massive destruction we pretend we don't see—is driven by a biological and not a cultural imperative[88]).

Animal behavior, they say, is fully driven by instinct. Animals—by which is meant all animals except humans—do not make conscious, rational decisions. They do not plan. They do not think. They are essentially machines made of DNA, guts, and fur, feathers, or scales.

Humans, they say, feel a wide range of emotions. Animals—by which is meant all animals except humans—do not. They do not grieve the loss of a mother, of freedom, of a world. They do not feel sorrow. They do not feel joy. They do not feel homesickness. They do not feel humiliated.

This culture believes that humans feel physical pain, but as with intelligence, animals—by which is meant all animals except humans—feel only a rudimentary pain, just sufficient to allow them to meaninglessly navigate their meaningless physical surroundings. Not long ago scientists conducted an experiment in which they injected bee venom or acetic acid into the lips of fish, after which "anomalous behaviors were exhibited." The scientists tortured fish to find out what we would all know if we paid any attention: that fish feel pain. The response by Bruno Broughton, a spokesperson for the United Kingdom's National Angling Alliance, was: "I doubt that it will come as much of a shock to anglers to learn that fish have an elaborate system of sensory cells around their mouths…. However, it is an entirely different matter to draw conclusions about the ability of fish to feel pain, a psychological experience for which they literally do not have the brains."[89] And just today I saw a news article about a videotape that was smuggled out of a kosher slaughterhouse. It reads: "Each animal is placed in a rotating drum so it [sic] can be killed while upside down, as required by Orthodox rabbis in Israel. Immediately after the ritual slaughterer, or *shochet,* has slit the throat, another worker tears open each steer's neck with a hook and pulls out the trachea and esophagus. The drum turns, and the steer is dumped on the floor. One after another, animals with dangling windpipes stand up or try to; in one case, death takes three minutes." The point? On seeing the tape, Rabbi Yisroel Belsky, one of the chief experts for the Orthodox Union, stated that the killings were certainly kosher, and moreover it was clear to him that each of the animals "felt nothing and that any motions it [sic] made were involuntary."[90]

This culture thinks that human life is sacred (at least some human life is sacred, but the lives of the poor, the nonwhite, the indigenous, as well as the lives of any who oppose the wishes of those in power are only a little sacred, or sometimes not sacred at all), but animal life is not sacred. In fact the entire animate world is not sacred.

Humans are the sole bearers of meaning, the sole definers of value, the only creatures capable of moral behavior. The lives of animals—all animals except humans—are utterly devoid of meaning. Their lives have no inherent value, in fact no value at all except insofar as that value is assigned to them by humans. This value is almost always strictly utilitarian. Most often this value is monetary, and more often than not this value is based not on their lives but on the price of their carcasses. And of course animals are incapable of moral behavior.

Finally, this culture constantly stresses that all that is human is good: humans have humanity and are humane, civilized are civil. Human traits are to be loved. Animal traits are to be hated, or rather hated traits are projected onto animals. Bad humans are animals, brutes, beasts, creatures. My Roget's thesaurus lists five synonyms for animal: *inferior, mindless, unthinking, intemperate, sensualist.* Mr. Roget forgot the word *it:* the words *who* or *whom* are almost never used for nonhuman animals, for the steer that (read *who*) is strapped to a rotating drum while its (read *his*) esophagus is ripped out, for the grizzly bears that (read *who*) will spend the rest of their lives in a tiny habitat (read *cage*) because they ate corn valued by humans at $20, for the rhinoceros mother that (read *who*) dies trying to protect its (read *her*) child.

The last bastion of defenders of zoos is nearly always the insistence that we must never anthropomorphize, that is, we must never "attribute human characteristics" to animals (by which is meant all animals except humans). This doesn't mean, of course, that we shouldn't perceive them as eagerly awaiting us. It doesn't mean that we shouldn't perceive them as being "bad girls" for "invading territory not their own." It doesn't mean we shouldn't perceive them as "couch potatoes." It doesn't mean we shouldn't perceive them as resembling "estate owners." It doesn't mean that the gorillas in ape heaven don't want to meet you. It means, quite simply, that we must do everything within our power to blind ourselves to their intelligence, their awareness, their feelings, their joys, their desires. It means we must blind ourselves to their *beingness,* their individuality, to *them,* to *who they are,* and to their value entirely independent of our own uses for them. It means most especially in this case that we must blind ourselves to their suffering.

WHAT DO WE REALLY LEARN FROM ZOOS? What do we learn looking at the pathetic, dejected, angry, or insane animals? What do we learn beyond the platitudes on the plaques in front of the bars, moats, or electrified fences?

We learn that humans are not animals. We learn that we are here and they are there. We learn that they are there for us, for our pleasure, our entertainment, our education: us. We learn that they have no existence independent of us. We learn that our world is limitless and their worlds are limited, constrained, constricted. We learn that we are more clever than they, or they would outwit us and escape. Or maybe that they do not want to escape, that the provision of bad food—the grizzlies in the San Francisco Zoo are now being fed commercial dog food—and concrete shelter within a cage is more important than freedom (the importance of having humans internalize this lesson for their own lives cannot be overstated). We learn that we are more powerful than they, or we could not confine them. We learn that it is acceptable for the technologically powerful to confine the less technologically powerful (once again, the importance of having especially less technologically powerful humans internalize this message cannot be overstated). We learn that each and every one of us, no matter how powerless we may feel in our own lives, is more powerful than the most mighty elephant or polar bear. Why? Because we can come, and we can go.

We learn that "habitat" is not unspoiled forests and plains and deserts and rivers and mountains and seas, but concrete cages with concrete rocks and the trunks of dead trees. We learn that "habitat" has sharp, immutable edges: everything inside the electrified fence is "bear habitat" and everything outside the fence is not. We learn that habitats do not meld and mix and flow back and forth over time. We learn that humans can make HABITAT™, and from that can come to believe that humans can make real habitat.

We learn that you can remove a creature from her habitat and still have a creature. We see a sea lion in a concrete pool and believe that we're still seeing a sea lion. But we are not. That is all wrong. We should never let zoologists define for us what or who an animal is. A sea lion is her habitat. She is the school of fish she chases. She is the water. She is the cold wind blowing over the ocean. She is the waves that strike the rocks on which she sleeps, and she is the rocks. She is the constant calling back and forth between members of her family, this talking to each other that never seems to stop. She is the shark who eventually ends her life. She is all of these things. She is that web. She is the process of being a sea lion, in place. She is her desires, which we can only learn by letting her show us, if she wants; not by encaging her.

We could and should say the same for every other creature, whether wolverine, gibbon, macaw, or elephant. I have a friend who has spent his life in the wild, and ecstatically reported to me one time that he saw a wolverine. I could have responded, "Big deal. I've seen plenty in zoos. They look like big weasels." But I have never seen a wolverine in the wild, which means I have never seen a wolverine.

Zoos teach us that animals are meat and bones in sacks of skin. You could put a wolverine into tinier and tinier cages, until you had a cage precisely the size of the wolverine, and you would still, according to what zoos implicitly teach, have a wolverine.

Zoos teach us that animals are like machine parts: separable, replaceable, interchangeable. They teach us that there is no web of life, that you can remove one part and put it into a box and still have that part. But that is all wrong. What is this wolverine? Who is this wolverine? What is her life really like? Not her life constrained by moats and walls, but her life in the forest, surrounded by that life, doing what wolverines do.

Zoos cannot teach us anything true about the lives of animals—not even human animals. They teach us that a wolverine/elephant/giraffe/anteater/grizzly bear/lion is a ridiculous animal pacing past its own shit in a cement cage. Zoos teach us implicitly that animals need to be managed, that they can't survive without us. They are our dependents, not our teachers, our neighbors, our betters, our equals, our friends, our gods. They are ours. We must assume the interspecies version of the white man's burden, and out of the goodness of our hearts we must benevolently control their lives. We must "rescue them from the wild."

Here is the real lesson taught by zoos, the ubiquitous lesson, the inescapable lesson, the overarching lesson, and really the only lesson that matters: a vast gulf separates humans and all other animals. It is wider than the widest moat, stronger than the strongest bars, more certain than the most lethal electric fence. We are here. They are there. We are special. We are separate.

The pretense that humans are superior to nonhumans is entirely unsupportable. I have seen no compelling evidence that humans are particularly more intelligent than any other creature. Surely the chimpanzee in the zoo was doing a better job of communicating than the human mothers who did not understand—or who did not allow themselves to understand—the communication she was trying to deliver. I have had long and fruitful relationships with many nonhuman animals, both domesticated and wild, and have reveled in the bouquet of radically different intelligences—different forms, not different "quantities"—which they have introduced to me, in his or her own time, each in his or her own way.

Similarly, I have seen no compelling evidence that animals do not plan, do not remember, do not hold grudges, do not gossip, do not squabble, do not have communities, do not grieve, do not feel joy, do not play games, do not make jokes, do not enjoy challenges, do not have fun, do not have morals, do not do or feel or think so many of the things that are so arrogantly deemed to be human traits. Indeed, I have seen all of these "human" traits in nonhuman animals.

A small example. Late the other night one of my dogs woke me with his barking. I stood and looked outside. It was a beautiful full moon night. I asked him to be quiet. He groaned and laid down. I went to bed. He started barking again. I got up again and asked him to be quiet. He groaned, walked in circles, and laid down. I went to bed. He started barking. I got up and yelled at him to shut up. He was quiet. The next morning when I got up he was gone. Later that day I walked to my mom's house. He was there. He wouldn't look at me. Normally he goes everywhere with me, but when I came home he demurred. It wasn't until the day after that he would look at me, and even then it was only after several apologies and a bunch of dog treats. Soon after that, however, I was forgiven.

I had no reason to get up early in the morning, and it was a beautiful night. There was no compelling reason for me to have to sleep right then in the first place. I don't see how the fact that I can type on a computer keyboard makes me any smarter in this case than a dog who at least has the sense to play in the moonlight.

This culture's unsupportable pretense that humans are superior to animals (and by now you know who is meant by this) leads within this culture to the equally unsupportable pretense that humans have the right—indeed, the mandate—to exploit animals (and also the vast majority of humans: the poor, women, nonwhites, the indigenous, and so on) in any way the exploiters see fit. If humans wish to encage animals for the entertainment of humans, humans have the unquestioned right to do so. And so on.

No, that last paragraph isn't quite true. I've reversed cause and effect. I do not believe that the notion that humans are superior leads to the notion that humans have the right to exploit those they consider beneath them. Instead the urge to exploit comes first, and justifications must be found to support this urge. Naked exploitation is rarely fully pleasing or sustainable to those perpetrating it. Exploitation is an empty substitute for relationship, at least as empty in its own way as spectacles. If spectacles substitute vicarious for direct experience and superficial identification for real relationship, exploitation involves taking by force what within a relationship might have been offered as a gift, which means it substitutes the taking of some tangible benefit for the building of a relationship. This means that exploitation will necessarily be as dissatisfying as spectacles, and for the same reasons. And because exploitation necessitates and leads to superficial relationships distant from the real beings of all participants, exploiters, analogous to consumers of spectacles, must also often ratchet up exerted control in order to stave off inevitable boredom, that is, to keep exploiters believing that they have experienced something, even if this belief lasts only for the short time of the act of exploitation itself.

Gifts form the core of mutual relationships. Much of the joy in these relationships is in the sparks in the spaces in between the participants, in the voluntary acts of giving and receiving time, energy, bodies, emotions, voices. Exploitation cuts these exchanges short, deprives them of their depth. Energy is still there, energy is still transferred, but it is shallow, empty, sharp.

An example may clarify. Let's say you and I are in love. Let's say you and I make love, give and receive each other's bodies, give and receive pleasure through our bodies, send and receive affection and meaning through our bodies, through our actions.

Now let's say we're not in love. Let's say I want to have you and you do not want to have me. You do not want to share yourself with me in that way. Now, let's say I take you anyway. I force myself on you. Certainly energy still passes between us. And I still feel a sort of pleasure. It doesn't much matter to me, on a fundamental level, whether you do or not, else I would have listened to you in the first place. But communication still takes place, although it is different than it would be if our intercourse were mutual.

You, at least, would be far more guarded, would give me far less of yourself than if it were mutual, and you would show me different parts of yourself in rape than in making love. You would not only close off much of the energy going out to me, but the energy that was coming out to me would be different: perhaps love in one case, perhaps hate and rage and sorrow in the other. And you would attempt to close off as much of my energy as possible coming in to you. You would receive less of me.

All of this leads to fundamentally insoluble problems for those who exploit (as well as, of course, for those they exploit). As with spectacles, when that deep organic flow of energy from relationship is cut off, it has to be made up somewhere. Certainly some of it can and does come from sucking the life of those they exploit. But still something feels wrong, feels empty. And so they must convince themselves that the other welcomes the exploitation, eagerly awaits the exploitation. But still that doesn't suffice, still they feel empty. And so now they must rationalize their behavior. They must attempt, desperately, incessantly, pathetically to normalize and moralize their behavior, to make others and especially themselves believe their behavior is both normal and moral, not exploitative.

How could it be exploitation if these others "literally don't have the brains" to know they're being exploited? How could it be exploitation if God gave us dominion over all these others, to subdue them, to master them? How could it be exploitation if evolution gave us dominion over all these others, because we're so damn smart? How can it be exploitation when humans are the sole bearers of meaning and the sole assigners of value? What we say goes. If we say it's not exploitation, well, by God and by evolution it's not. How can it be exploitation when animals are here solely for human pleasure?

It really isn't exploitation. Humans really aren't animals. Animals really can't think or feel.

Just keep saying that over and over.

But even if you do, in the end it still won't help. Spectacles and exploitation are both parodies, toxic mimics, of real relationships, taking on the form and perverting the content. As such they can never provide what we are missing but sometimes don't even know we miss; what we need but sometimes don't even know we need.

You cannot cure loneliness with spectacles or exploitation. You can make yourself forget for a very short time, but the emptiness will come back. It will always come back.

HUMANS EVOLVED EMBEDDED IN THE NATURAL WORLD. It is our real and only home. Deep, abiding, and embodied relationships with wild and wildly varied intelligences are part of who we are, part of who we must be. They form us, teach us how to act, how to think, how to perceive, how to be. They are and have from the beginning been who we are. What is true for sea lions and wolverines is no less true for human beings. We are our habitat. We need our habitat. If we are removed from our habitat, if living, breathing, wild, intelligent habitat is replaced with walls, we will go insane, no matter how much phony "enrichment" we have. We will

exhibit strange repetitive behaviors. We might, for example, fabricate 13.5 quadrillion lethal doses of plutonium-239. We might build two million dams in the United States, and across the world we might erect one dam per hour, every hour, day and night, compulsively stopping rivers. We might change the climate. We might destroy the ozone layer. We might contaminate every stream in the United States with carcinogens, and then continue to fabricate and distribute more. We might destroy life on the planet, yet pay more attention to professional sporting events and the romantic liaisons of famous people—the enrichments provided for us in our walled cells. We might destroy our children; it is no wonder that civilized humans—those deprived of deep and daily relationships with their natural habitat—abuse their children. Placement in zoos, or forced removal from one's natural, necessary habitat, which includes one's natural, necessary social nexus, causes reproductive disturbances. What's true for pandas and flamingos is true for humans.

Honestly, bad food and concrete walls cannot substitute for freedom and relationships. For that matter, good food and concrete canyons of skyscrapers cannot substitute for freedom and relationships.

Years ago I interviewed John A. Livingston, author of the extraordinary book *The Fallacy of Wildlife Conservation.* I quoted back to him something he'd written, "I believe we live in a society of sensory deprivation, with all the bizarre imaging that that implies."

He responded, "Nowadays most of us live in cities. That means that most of us live in an insulated cell, completely cut off from any kind of sensory information or sensory experience that is not of our own manufacture. All the sensory information we receive is *fabricated,* and most of it is mediated by machines.

"I think the only thing that makes it bearable is the fact that our sensory capacities are so terribly diminished—just as they are in all domesticates—that we no longer know what we're missing. The wild animal is receiving information from all his or her senses, from an uncountable number of sources, every moment of its life. We get it from one only—ourselves. It's like doing solitary in an echo chamber.

"People doing solitary do strange things. And the common experience of victims of sensory deprivation is hallucination. I believe that our received cultural wisdom, our anthropocentric beliefs and ideologies, can easily be seen as institutionalized hallucinations."[91]

Livingston expands on this: "This society is of course the spawn of its environment (the interaction of its culture and itself). Our present predicament has entirely cultural roots. The tradition out of which we have come has, by a process of artificial selection as sophisticated and complex as that of any geneticist, produced a cultivar so remote from its origins that they are barely discernible. We have been unceremoniously ripped from our life context, sprayed in plastic, and packaged in hermetically sealed containers. Sealed off from our aliveness, including our sensory processes. All this has been done through cultural conditioning. We have been divorced for so long not only from biophysical nature but also from the very awareness of biophysical nature that our images of the world and even of ourselves have become little more than institutionalized hallucinations."

He continues, "Our culture has institutionalized such hallucinatory images as human supremacy over all animate and inanimate nature; a swollen, obese GNP as the very model of social health; high technology as the Holy Grail, and so on. There is even a picture of a planned, organized, ordered, and thus understandable and manageable universe. The trouble with all of these counterfeit bubblegum cards is that there is no external 'real world' opposite number with which to match them. They are displayed into emptiness; they are without meaning. They are, in my view, precisely the sorts of hallucinations that arise in sensory deprivation, in the absence of natural sensory stimuli. If perceiving really is hypothesis testing, then many of our most treasured hypotheses are not testing out.

"So it is, I think, that our perceptions (and our concepts) having to do with man and nature and the cosmos, are images that reflect the 'real thing' about as accurately as toy poodles with painted claws resemble the wolf, as assembly-line leghorns resemble the real jungle fowl, as glazed castrated Herefords swimming in drugs resemble the great white aurochs. The image no longer matches the reality. Our culture sees to it that sensory impressions from the natural world are consistently screened from us, so that both as individuals and as societies we are permitted to perceive only distorted images of our own queer, tortured, internal fabrication.

"In this sense our hallucinations about the relationship between man and non-man, for example, become understandable. By closing off our connections with external reality, which happens to be our root system, our culture drives us to dependence on entirely artificial support. We are left with a jumbled catch-bag of monstrous illusions, and what is more, we take our hallucinations for truth. Seeing is believing. Even more important, believing is seeing."[92]

What do you see when you go to a zoo? Do you see animals? Do you see cages? What—or whom—do you see?

A ZOO IS NOT MERELY A NIGHTMARE taking shape in concrete and steel. It is the forced importation of wild animals into the no-longer beating heart of the ongoing nightmare—hallucination—that is this deathly culture, this culture that is killing the planet.

Each new creature forced or born into a zoo is a retelling of the story of each human forced or born into this culture. Each new human forced or born into this culture is a retelling of the story of each new creature forced or born into a zoo. It is the nightmare story of the culture itself, the nightmare story of walls closing in.

The modernization of zoo cages and their renaming as "habitat" fits perfectly into the story of our own confinement. Modern cages—the kind in zoos—use fewer bars, not because moats or electrified fences provide more freedom for those encaged, but because they provide the illusion of freedom to those who watch. The fantasy of the consumers of the spectacle, the fantasy of the consumers of the animals—the fantasy that the animals are eagerly awaiting us, awaiting our use—will be slightly less brittle. As the real world is increasingly consumed and turned into artificial habitat, or rather HABITAT™, for humans and nonhumans alike, we increasingly attempt to blur the distinction between habitat and HABITAT™, until multiple authors can state with a presumably straight face that the whole world is a zoo. All of this helps us forget what we have lost, and what we are continuing to lose. This helps us forget who we are meant to be, who we are, and what we have become. As we become increasingly metabolized into the system, as we increasingly forget that we are animals who need habitat, we no longer need bars, nor even moats nor electrified fences, to contain us. We contain ourselves in our offices, in our houses, in front of our television sets, in our cities. And we pretend we are still free. We pretend we are still alive.

For the most part modern zoos provide more "enrichment" than old-style menageries (though of course the animals are still not free). This too has a human equivalent, as those of us closer to the center of civilization have far more "enrichments" to help us pass the time, "enrichments" that are utterly unnecessary when living in the real world.

I do not believe that the pacing bear driven mad would now leave her cell even if she could. If returned to her home she would probably not know what to do. Neither do we. This means the barriers that separate us from freedom can now be more hidden from superficial view.

What is true for bears, penguins, and boa constrictors is true for humans. Just because we pretend our own barriers to freedom are not there does not mean our pretense is real. We are still not free. We are no longer able to interact with our habitat, which means we are no longer who we are. We are no longer human.

Another argument put forward by those in favor of zoos is that zoos are immensely popular entertainment. In North America, for example, more people visit zoos than go to all professional sports events combined.[93]

At $10 to $20 dollars a head to get through the door, along with another $8 for parking, $6 for "zoo burgers," "rhino shakes," and "monkey fries,"[94] and $12 for a stuffed furry toy animal, it becomes clear that zoos are staggeringly big business. Perhaps it becomes clear, too, why zookeepers refuse to empathize with the animals they incarcerate: Who was it who said, "It is difficult to get a man to understand something when his salary depends on his not understanding it"?[95]

It would be easy enough to explore the power relationships made manifest by the immense popularity of zoos. Within a culture organized so completely and fundamentally on hierarchical ways of perceiving the world and being in the world, it can be a tremendous relief—and great fun, in a sad sort of way—for those who are essentially powerless, whose own lives are so desperately out of control (and in a world being killed as we watch television, flipping faster and faster through the channels and trying so very hard to find something—anything—that will hold our attention and make the miserable, lonely time pass just a little bit faster, all our lives are by definition out of control), to get to look at those whose lives are even more wretched than ours, more out of their control, more tedious, more helpless.

Although I'm certain that this accounts for a good portion of the popularity of zoos, and a good portion of the cruelty associated with zoos, I'm equally certain that there are also other, perhaps more interesting, factors in zoos' popularity.

Just today I was speaking with Robert Shetterly, the painter responsible for the powerful collection of portraits entitled Americans Who Tell the Truth. I told him about this book, about trying to find the reasons for zoos' popularity. He said, "When I was a child I always both loved and hated zoos. I loved them because I got to see real live animals, as opposed to animals on television, and I hated them because the animals were so obviously unhappy."[96]

There you have it. This was my own childhood experience of zoos, and this has been the response by nearly everyone to whom I've mentioned this book.

It's a cliché among pro-zoo books, by the way, for the authors to state that the responses of their friends were similar to the responses of mine in that whenever they'd mention they were writing a book on zoos, their friends would say something to the effect of, "I hope you're in favor of shutting those horrid things down." At this point the pro-zoo authors would inevitably do the literary equivalent of a heavy sigh, and then with great patience—as well as smugness—explain why zoos are not only great places in their own right but why they are necessary and beneficial for the animals themselves. The real point of their discussion, and this is the point of so much discourse within this culture, is to lead people away from their own instinctual feelings, their own revulsion at what is so obviously wrong, their empathy for the suffering of others, and to lead them to trust experts: "Oh, I thought I hated zoos, but I guess he's writing a book on zoos, and so obviously he must know more than I. Maybe zoos are necessary and good after all."

CHILDREN, IT ENDS UP, are the usual instigators of zoo visits.[97] Children, more even than most of us, require connections with nonhuman others. This accounts for some of the popularity of teddy bears (and teddy alligators, aardvarks, anteaters, elephants, monkeys, and so on), as well as books illustrated with animals, animated films starring nonhuman animals, and wildlife murals for children.

Baratay and Hardouin-Fugier observe, "Children's attention at the zoo is most focused when they are between the ages of four and ten. When younger, they tend to see only smaller animals (pigeons, sparrows); when older, they lose interest in the subject to some extent. Between four and ten, however, they project their own imaginary bestiaries onto the animals they see, who thus serve as illustrations of a sort of virtual reality. Children begin by examining animals' morphologies, remarking on their characteristic traits (trunk, neck, hump) and using their own experience to identify them. They ask their names or give them names of their own. The youngest children (four to six years) speak to animals and assign them places in a human universe (house, daddy, mommy), preferring species that [sic] look like their plush toys." I would say instead that children prefer those species who look familiar. If you know wild animals you will connect with wild animals. If all you know is plush toys then you will only be capable of connecting with animals these plush toys resemble (exemplifying John Livingston's point about being in solitary confinement, with no references save those of human origin). Baratay and Hardouin-Fugier continue, "Older children choose those that [sic] correspond to the heroes of their books and films, and attribute similar characteristics to them. Some writers discern in this a dulling of animal imagery and a failure to appreciate the reality of nature, which is in fact cruel [sic] and entirely focused on the fight for survival [sic]. But this perception is just as false; children are merely amplifying the anthropocentric vision of adults."[98]

As much as I appreciate so much of Baratay and Hardouin-Fugier's work, they missed the boat on this one. They are correct in stating that writers are wrong when they say that children do not appreciate "the reality of nature, which is in fact cruel and entirely focused on the fight for survival," but not for the reason they probably think. The writers who believe "nature" is cruel and animals are "entirely focused on the fight for survival" have spent too much time with capitalists and not enough time with wild animals. They are just plain wrong, and guilty of the worst sort of projection: pretending that the whole world is as cruel, exploitative, and unfriendly as this culture. This culture frantically insists that all cultures are based on violence, that all cultures destroy their landbase, that men of all cultures rape women, that children of all cultures are beaten, that the poor of all cultures are forced to pay rent to the rich (or even that all cultures have rich and poor!), that all cultures incarcerate animals. Perhaps the best example of this culture trying to naturalize its violence is the belief that natural selection is based on competition, and that all survival is a violent struggle where only the meanest, most exploitative survive. The fact that this belief is nearly ubiquitous in this culture, despite it being demonstrably untrue and logically untenable, reveals the degree to which we have lost our senses in the echo chamber that is this culture. If you let me use a couple of semicolons, I can disprove the notion that competition drives natural selection in one sentence: Those creatures who have survived in the long run have survived in the long run; if you hyperexploit your surroundings you will deplete them and die off (as we shall soon see with industrialized humans); the only way to survive in the long run is to give back more than you take, to improve your habitat. Instead of survival of the fittest, it's survival of the fit: how well you fit into your habitat, how much better you make it, on its own terms, by your existence. The deer and the wolf work together to make them both stronger, faster. This understanding of the fundamentally cooperative—and joyful—nature of reality is directly in line with many indigenous, noncivilized, wild cosmologies.

A few years ago, American Indian writer Vine Deloria said to me, in words that reveal the absolute contrast between the echo chamber into which we in our culture have confined ourselves and the relationship most humans throughout time have entered into with their surroundings, "What happens in the different Indian religions is that people live so intimately with their environment that they enter into relationship to the spirits that live in particular places. Rather than an article of faith, it's part of human experience. And I think non-Indians sometimes experience this also when they spend a long time in one place.

"Living in this universe, Indians believed that everything humans experience has value, and instructs us in some aspect of life. Because everything is alive and making choices that determine the future, the world is constantly creating itself, and because every moment brings something new, we need to always try to not classify things too quickly. All the data must be considered, and we need to try to find how the ordinary and the extraordinary come together, as they must, in one coherent, comprehensive, mysterious story line. With the wisdom and time for reflection that old age brings, we may discover unsuspected relationships that make themselves manifest in our consciousness and so come to be understood.

"In this moral universe, all activities, events, and entities are related, and so it doesn't matter what kind of existence an entity enjoys—whether it is human or otter or star or rock—because the responsibility is always there for it to participate in the continuing creation of reality. Life is not a predatory jungle, 'red in tooth and claw,' as Westerners like to pretend, but is better understood as a symphony of mutual respect in which each player has a specific part to play. We must be in our proper place and we must play our role at the proper moment. So far as humans are concerned, because we came last, we are the 'younger brothers and sisters' of the other life-forms, and therefore have to learn everything from these other creatures. The real interest of old Indians would then be not to discover the abstract structure of physical reality, but rather to find the proper road down which, for the duration of a person's life, that person is supposed to walk."[99]

The projection that the world is "cruel and entirely focused on the fight for survival" reveals far more about the psyches of those who claim it than it does about physical reality.

Further, I do not believe that, as Baratay and Hardouin-Fugier say, "children are merely amplifying the anthropocentric vision of adults." Quite the opposite: I think that instead they have not yet been fully inculcated into this culture's anthropocentric—narcissistic—mindset. They've not yet forgotten their kinship to nonhuman others, not yet had that vital bond severed between themselves and the wild. Some have not yet become convinced that nonhuman animals have nothing to teach us.

Humans visit zoos because we *need* contact with wild animals. We need wild animals to remind us of the enormous complexity of life, to remind us that the world was *not* made just for us, to remind us that we are *not* the center of the universe. We need them to teach us how to live.

As I said before, children need this contact even more than do adults. It is no coincidence that most zoo visits are instigated by children, nor that children are interested in animals' anatomical features and names.

The ethologist Paul Shepard thought and wrote about this a lot, writing, for example, "One of the most astonishing aspects of language [in humans] is its ties to the personal calendar. The unfolding process, starting with the yearling, is as tightly regimented as a fire drill: cooing, lallation, babbling, single nouns, adverbs, conjunctions, all in their time…. Primary language learning is scheduled to be basically complete in the individual by the age of four. Yet the kind and amount of communication as speech done by four-year-olds hardly seems to demand language at all…. Whatever could evolution have been thinking of, to rig our personal time-tables so as to put words in the mouths of babes?"

He answers his own question: "Speech is the means by which category-making proceeds, representing things that could be pyramided and stacked in memory by classifying…. Thinking is, of course, far more than naming, categorizing, and recalling, but these are basic to it. The meaning of words is straightforward for the child. The subtleties of symbolism, serendipities of insight, and the permutations of ideas are of great value, but they are only potential for the individual if he has a proper infancy of mundane name learning.

"As surely as he 'learns' to walk, the two-year-old begins to demand the names of things. By vocal imitation and repetition, he begins a compulsive collecting of kinds that will go on for a decade. The process has that inexorable quality of the growth of plant tendrils, and one can almost feel the neural cells putting down rootlets that organize the soil spaces beneath them."[100]

His point is that human children have an innate need to categorize, an imperative as natural, strong, undeniable, and fundamental as the cutting of teeth. This seeing, hearing, experiencing, and categorizing is crucial to every child's development of the abilities to think, to reflect, and ultimately to gain wisdom and to understand the roles we are to play in the larger symphony of life.

But why nonhuman animals? Why can't children simply learn to think by categorizing types of cars, or memorizing presidents, or learning baseball statistics?

Recalling for a moment John Livingston's description of humans doing solitary confinement in an echo chamber should give us the answer: we need those others to keep our thinking from becoming purely self-referential—narcissistic—and we need them to keep us grounded, to remind us who we are and why we're here. Years ago Paul Shepard told me, "Once frogs and salamanders and condors are gone, and we have nothing in their place but our sheep and stupid cows and horses—horses who have become our model for horsepower and therefore for dominance—when we have nothing left but those, there will be no evidence that we are not actually the purpose of the whole thing—a delusion. There will be no true otherness in the world to keep us both sane and small."[101]

But there's far more to it, as Shepard makes clear:

"Mentally and emotionally, children, juveniles, and adolescents move through a world that is structured around them following a time-layered sequence of mother and other caregivers, nature, and cosmos. Infants go from their own and their mother's body to exploring the body of the earth to the body of the cosmos…. The study of nature among primitives begins in childhood but is a lifelong preoccupation.

"The most crucial human experience is childhood—its bonding, socializing, and exploration of the nonhuman world, its naming and identification. Speech emerges according to an intrinsic timetable. Language must be taught. But nature is the child's tangible basis upon which symbolic meanings will be posited."[102]

This is why children want—need—to go to zoos: they understand in their bodies the developmental necessity of being in the presence of wild animals. They understand—but of course cannot articulate—that to fail to enter into these relationships with nonhuman others—whether because the children live in cities, which are inimical to most animals; or because the ideology handed down by their elders proclaims nonhumans beneath any other than utilitarian consideration—is to take a major and often irreversible step into the delusion-inducing echo chamber of human-centered thought. If "nature is the child's tangible basis upon which symbolic meanings will be posited," and if the child does not experience nature, the child—and later the adult will have a warped sense of meaning.

As we see.

Yesterday, page A18 of the *San Francisco Chronicle* carried an article about how global warming is proceeding much more quickly than anyone feared. That's page A18. Page A1 contained a story entitled, "Silicon Valley loses fight on stock options: Companies must deduct perk's value when figuring profit." Then today an article buried in the bowels of the newspaper revealed—no big surprise here—that the U.S. government refuses to do anything to halt or even slow global warming because to do so would possibly harm the economy.

A warped sense of meaning.

The implications are extreme. It's not too much to say, as

does Dolores LaChapelle, author of *Sacred Land Sacred Sex: Rapture of the Deep*, that "the roots of our environmental destructiveness lie in a failed development of the self. Before the modern era, for [hundreds of] thousands of years, children played freely in wild nature. Adolescents became adults through nature myths and rituals that took place in a community that included both humans and the more-than-human world surrounding them."[103]

Shepard writes, "Picture the circumstances of growing up today, surrounded not only by domestic as opposed to wild things but also being encased continuously in structures and landscapes that are the creations of human beings. Our lawns of domesticated plants, and the very laying out of streets and the enclosing of space by buildings, engenders the illusion we've created the world. That kind of imprint, using this word in the Lorenzian sense of semi-irreversible knowledge acquired extremely early in life, lends itself to the notion that indeed a humanlike deity somewhere created this world very much as we create towns [or zoos]. And did it for our use."[104]

Welcome to the world of zoos.

But another world is possible. The world where we evolved. The world not made for us. The world we're made for. I'm going to return to Paul Shepard twice more. First, he expands on the work of the anthropologist Claude Lévi Strauss by saying, "The 'savage mind' grasps the world in a totality of present and past with all its multiplicity and complexity. On the other hand, as Lévi Strauss has revealed, civilized thought attempts to simplify rather than clarify the complexity of the world. It does so by unifying and seeking continuity, variability, and relativity rather than by conceptualizing new schemes, as does 'savage' thought, that then become additional objects to be comprehended. Stated simply, the 'civilized mind' attempts to simplify and level the world whereas the 'savage mind' is not afraid to become enmeshed in its complexity."[105]

Zoos are a manifestation of this civilizing process: the foreclosure of options, the enclosure of freedoms, the simplification of everyone and everything. A bear is simplified to meat in a sack of brown fur, and not the relationships, desires, and behaviors that *make* a bear. She becomes a BEAR™. Habitat is simplified from endless prairies, glens, mountains, and streamsides to a concrete box with tires on the floor, or maybe ten thousand square feet of dirt, grass, and oh, yes, as always walls. This is part of the sorrow of a visit to a zoo.

AGAIN: ANOTHER WAY of perceiving the world is possible. I quote Paul Shepard one last time as he cites musicologist Marina Roseman's work with the Temiar, who are "a rain-forest people of the Malay peninsula whose culture is filled with song and spirituality. 'Instead of alienating flowers, trees, or cicadas as inherently different and distant,' she says, 'the Temiar stress an essential similarity.' The Temiar 'receive inspiration and constant regeneration from interactions with the essences of mountains, rivers, fruits, and creatures of the tropical rain forest…. Temiar culture is an exquisite translation of the natural environment into cultural terms. The jungle is a social space.' The emphasis on place is central to their music. The forest is a reflection of social relationships mediated by song. 'If we compare at the level of segmentary, nonhierarchical societies adapted to tropical forest environments,' says Roseman, 'two features become apparent. One concerns mutualistic responses to the rain-forest environment; the other, modes of political persuasion that are influential and cooperative rather than authoritarian and coercive.'"[106]

Our separation from the natural world affects every aspect of our lives, from the most intimate to the most global.

There is another part to the sorrow inherent in visiting a zoo. In addition to our empathetic response to the suffering of another—to the degree that we have any empathy left— there is the visceral realization that we are seeing shells. And perhaps more to the point, we are simply seeing these individual and isolated shells as opposed to enmeshing ourselves in a web of complex relationships and mutual respect. Seeing these shells of animals in parodies of habitat will of course make us sad, and even more lonely than before we arrived. These animals—these shells of animals— remind us of what we've lost, and what we're losing even more with every day that passes. It is not possible to "receive inspiration and constant regeneration from interactions with the essences of" our nonhuman brothers and sisters when those essences are absent.

And that's a big part of the problem. A child who goes to a zoo is not encountering real animals. Like any other spectacle, like any other pornography, a zoo can never really satisfy, can never really deliver what it promises.

Zoos commit at least four unforgivable sins. First, they destroy the lives of those they cage. Second, they destroy our understanding of who and what animals and habitats really are. Third, they destroy our understanding of who and what we really are. And fourth, they destroy the potential for mutual relationships, not only with those particular encaged animals but also with those still wild.

Zoos—like pornography, like science—substitute superficial relationships based on hierarchy, based on dominance and submission, based on a detached consumer manipulating and observing another who may or may not have given permission to be the object of this gaze, for deep relationships based on mutual respect and the giving of gifts.

Think of a pornographic picture. Even in cases where women are paid and willingly pose for pornography, they have not given me permission to see their bodies—or rather images of their bodies—right here right now. If I have a photograph, I have it forever, even if subsequently the woman withdraws her permission. This is the opposite of relationship, where the woman can present herself to me now, and now, and now, always at both her and my and our discretion (and of course I can present myself to her now, and now, and now, also always at her and my and our discretion). What in the latter case is a moment by moment gift becomes in the former case my property, to do with as I choose. This is, of course, true of all photographs.

And it is true of zoos. I do not and cannot command the bear whose home I share to appear before me. Nor the gray jays, the slender salamanders, the slugs. They are willful and independent.

Everything is far worse than I am making it seem. Zoos—like pornography, like science, like other toxic mimics—take a very real, necessary, creative, life-affirming, and most of all relational urge and turn it—pervert it—until it furthers not fully mutual relationships at all but instead superficial relationships based on domination and control. Indeed, zoos—like pornography, like science, like other toxic mimics—can cause people to forget those original relational urges, to forget mutuality is possible, to forget depth is possible, to believe control is natural and desirable. Pornography takes the creative relational need for sexuality with a willing partner—and the intimacy this can imply—and simplifies it to the relationship of watcher and watched. Science takes the creative relational need for understanding and the gaining of wisdom and simplifies it to that same dynamic; watcher and watched; dominator and dominated; subject and object.[107] Zoos take the creative need for participating in relationships with wild nonhuman others and simplify it until our "nature experience" consists of spending a few moments looking at—or simply walking by—insane bears and angry chimpanzees in concrete cages.

Incarcerating animals in zoos is to entering into relationships with them in the wild as rape is to making love. The former in each case requires coercion, limits the freedom of the victim, springs from, manifests, and reinforces self-perceived entitlement to full access to the victim on the part of the perpetrator. The former in each case damages the ability of both victim and perpetrator to enter into future intimate relationships. It distorts the notion of what constitutes a relationship. It is based on the dyad of dominance and submission. It closes off any possibility for real and willing understanding of the other.

The latter in each case is a dance among willing participants who give what they wish as they wish when they wish. It inspires present and future intimacy, present and future understanding of the other and the self. It nourishes those involved. It makes us more of who we are.

Portfolio Three

IMPRISONED

Grévy's zebra, *Equus grevyi*: Eastern Africa

California sea lion, *Zalophus californianus:* Northern Pacific Ocean

Snowy owl, *Bubo scandiacus*: Circumpolar, Arctic regions

Kit fox, *Vulpus macrotis:* Southwest North America, northern Mexico

Polar bear, *Ursus maritimus:* Arctic regions of Alaska, Canada, Greenland, Norway, Russia

Raccoon, *Procyon lotor*: North America, introduced into continental Europe

Painted stork (Indian wood ibis), *Mycteria leucocephala:*
Cambodia, eastern China, India, Pakistan, Sri Lanka, Vietnam

Cuban crocodile, *Crocodylus rhombifer*: Cuba

Trumpeter swan, *Olor buccinator*: North America

Guanacos, *Lama guanicoe:* Argentina, Chile, southern Peru

Snow leopard, *Uncia uncia* or *Panthera uncia*: Mountains of central Asia

South American condor, *Vultur gryphus:* Western South America

Okapi, *Okapia johnstoni:* Ituri rainforest of the Democratic Republic of the Congo

White rhinoceros, *Ceratotherium simum:* Northeastern and southern Africa

Arctic fox (white phase), *Alopex lagopus:* Circumpolar, alpine Iceland and Scandinavia

Western lowland gorilla, *Gorilla gorilla gorilla:* Angola, Cameroon,
Central African Republic, Democratic Republic of the Congo, Gabon, Republic of Equitorial Guinea

Bactrian camel, *Camelus bactrianus:* Northwest China, Mongolia

Kodiak bear (Alaskan brown bear), *Ursus arctos middendorffi*: Southern Alaska

Black bear, *Ursus americanus:* North America, Mexico

Puma (cougar, mountain lion), *Puma concolor:* North and South America

Mandrill, *Mandrillus sphinx*: Cameroon, Democratic Republic of the Congo, Gabon, Republic of Equitorial Guinea

Takin, *Budorcas taxicolor*: Eastern Himalayas, Bhutan, China, Myanmar

African lion, *Panthera leo:* East and southern Africa

Great horned owl, *Bubo virginianus:* North, Central, and South America

Western lowland gorillas, *Gorilla gorilla gorilla:* Angola, Cameroon,
Central African Republic, Democratic Republic of the Congo, Gabon, Republic of Equitorial Guinea

I AM NOT GENERALLY KNOWN for presenting tangible solutions to the problems we face. This is because for the most part these problems are symptoms of and endemic to deeper psychological and perceptual faults, which means "solving" a problem technically without addressing these underlying faults will simply cause the pathology to present itself in a different way.

That said, I think I see a straightforward solution to the problem of children needing encounters with wild animals and zoos providing parodies of these encounters, in so doing deforming children's perception and understanding of human–nonhuman relationships, causing children to perceive themselves as separate from and superior to nonhuman animals.

This solution is predicated, of course, on the probably unrealistic assumption that parents *want* their children to perceive themselves as embedded in and a part of their landbase, and *not* as separate from or superior to it.

The solution is let your child explore nature. I'm not talking about getting in the car and heading up to hang with all the other tourists at Yosemite, effectively exchanging your city-based traffic jam for a "nature-based" traffic jam, although the latter will probably have more beautiful scenery outside your windows. To drive through nature is not all that different from being surrounded on four sides by movie screens as the visuals of a road rush up to greet you. Throw in the rocking of the car and toss some pine-scented freshener into the air vents and the simulation will be more or less complete: you might even think you're there.

Hiking is not all that much better. You're still a tourist. No matter how spectacular Yosemite or Yellowstone or the Grand Canyon are, they're still spectacles unless you live there. Unless you call it your home. Unless it says it's your home.

I'm talking about staying home.

When Vine Deloria told me about the grand symphony of mutual respect, we also talked about living in place. I began by quoting to him something the Osage chief Big Soldier once said, "I see and admire your manner of living… In short you can do almost what you choose. You whites possess the power of subduing almost every animal to your use. You are surrounded by slaves. Every thing about you is in chains and you are slaves yourselves. I fear that if I should exchange my pursuits for yours, I too should become a slave."

Vine responded, "That's the best thing any Indian ever said, and I think it applies straight across the board. I teach at the University of Colorado, and so many of the students are convinced that they are free because they act just like each other. They all do the same things. They think alike. They're almost like a herd, or like they've all been cloned. They're enslaved to a certain way of life. Once you've traded away spiritual insight for material comfort, it is extremely difficult to ever get back to any sense of authenticity. You see these poor kids going out hiking in the mountains, trying to commune with nature, and yet you can't commune with nature just taking a walk. You have to actually live it. And these young people have no way of critiquing the society that is enslaving them, because the only experiences they're really going to have are the occasional weekend hikes. They may see beautiful vistas, and they may get a sense of this other aesthetic, but they're not going to get to the metaphysical sense of who they really are. In this sense, Appalachian whites, rural blacks, and Scandinavian farmers are all so much closer to the natural world because they live in it twenty-four hours a day. These groups may not see themselves as a single group, yet they are all connected by their oppression by industrialization, by the destruction of the landbases on which their lives depend, and by their connection to the natural world that teaches them who they are. And it's not just an abstract connection to an abstract earth, but instead what is important is the relationship you have with a particular tree or a particular mountain."[108]

Although I traveled extensively as a child—hitting forty-nine states, all but one of the Canadian provinces, and every American country as far south as Nicaragua, all before I was ten—I gained my love of nature, learned how to think, name, and categorize, gained the tangible basis upon which symbolic meanings were to be posited, and for that matter discovered who I was mainly in the window-wells and backyard of my home, and beyond that in a pasture, and beyond that in an irrigation ditch. I learned far more from the toads and salamanders who lived in the window-wells than I did from all the vacations, all the hikes, all the back-packing, all the four-wheeling, and yes, all the visits to natural history museums and zoos (both of which seemed even at the time to be neither more nor less than mau-soleums, one bona fide, the other only slightly premature). I learned from the grasses, ants, and grasshoppers in the pasture, the snakes and crawdads in the irrigation ditch. The lessons and encounters weren't all that extraordinary. And that is precisely the point. We were just neighbors.

I can hear your voice already, somewhat incredulous, "Don't go to a zoo?" you ask, "Just go outside? That's boring."

Good, I respond. Boredom, like confusion, can be a good state. So long as you're not being manipulated, confusion merely means you're thinking about something you've never before thought of. You're lost, and you've yet to find your way. Similarly, so long as you're not artificially confined, boredom simply means you've not yet found what you want to do. You're lost, just as with confusion, and you've yet to find your way. As such, boredom, like confusion, can be an important preparatory step toward new understanding or action, so long as the process isn't prematurely aborted—that is, so long as you have the courage and patience to not bail out too early. If you're bored and you don't like the feeling, you'll soon enough find something to do. Or maybe someone will find you to say hello. In fact, I don't think it's too much to say that boredom plus freedom often leads to creativity.[109]

Joseph Campbell said I think something similar, though in a far more scholarly way: "And absolutely indispensable for any such development is that *separation* from the demands of the day which all educators—until recently—understood to be the first requirement for anything approaching a spiritual life."[110] Separation from the demands of the day equals leisure equals time to get bored equals time to pass through being bored to come to understand what you want to do.

Boredom—when one is not confined (I am explicitly excluding human and nonhuman prisoners)—can also be simply a slowing down. We are so accustomed, from zoos, from nature programs, from television in general and even more generally from the speed of this culture, to things happening on command. I send an email and I want it to arrive in Bangkok right now. I turn on the television and I want to see a movie right now. But snakes and spiders run on their own time, a slower time. If you see a spider on a nature program, you're pretty much guaranteed she will kill something—or rather, someone—during her few moments of screen time. But just right now I'm looking at spiders on my wall and ceiling. The spiders are sitting, sitting, sitting. They sit for hours, sometimes days. I often wonder what they're thinking. I'll probably never know. I certainly won't know unless they tell me. And even if they tell me I won't perceive it unless I'm paying attention, and unless I've learned at least a little of their language. And that, once again, is precisely the point.

Hummingbirds and whirligig beetles, too, run on different time. Theirs seems a faster time, as they're always moving, spinning, doing something. They always seem breathless, or maybe it's just that watching them makes me lose my own breath. And what are the hummingbirds thinking as they swoop above my head, chirping? What are the whiriligig beetles contemplating as they dance? It's the same answer as with the spiders, and the same crucial point.

As children know, boredom is a non-issue anyway. The one time as a child I came in from the pasture to complain to my mom I was bored, she said, "Good. Why don't you clean the dirty dishes in the sink? After that the garden needs weeding, and after that…" It worked. I never again complained of boredom.

Now I can hear your voice again. This time you say, "That's all very good for you, Mr. Hayseed Goatroper Country Boy, but what about those of us who live in cities? Your idea doesn't do shit—something else you're probably familiar with—for us."

I responded to this question while sitting on the grass in between Highway 101 and the McDonald's parking lot. I wanted to go to the outdoor place in this town that was the least hospitable to life and see what I would see. It was a tough choice. Wal-Mart or McDonald's, which is more toxic? I drove in to town, stopping by the post office. At first all I noticed was the large number of apes, this being five days before Christmas. They were of the genus *Homo,* species *sapiens sapiens* (the second *sapiens* added by taxonomists to make sure we get the joke). Some consider them a class of animal entirely separate from all others, called, I believe, *Homo supremus supremus supremus maximus* but more accurately labeled *Homo domesticus.* It's always been clear to me, however, that they are simply *Homo sapiens* [sic], apes wearing clothes, and in this case standing in line to mail Christmas presents.

But then a fly landed on my backpack, and stayed with me all through the line. Even when I pulled my checkbook from the pack the fly didn't leave, but walked away from my hand. From the post office I went to the bank. More apes there, but the fly still hung out on my pack. I went back to my truck, and on to the McDonald's parking lot.

I have to admit that when I got here things looked pretty bleak, even boring. More apes, of course, but they're so common that sometimes I don't even notice them anymore. The only interesting thing I saw at first was a circle A for anarchy on a concrete wall, but that's just another human symbol. I plopped down on the grass near some weeds waving in the winter wind, and considered giving up my project before it started. I didn't think anyone (except for the grasses, water and wind) would be here. But soon I noticed the tiniest red flower on a short and slender green stalk, and the shoots of other plants preparing for next spring. No animals, though. Then suddenly a giant bumblebee crawled from beneath the weeds, made her way under and over twigs to the edge of the grass, began flying, circled the weeds two or three times, and took off to the east, over the top of the McDonald's. Something clicked inside, and I was able to see and hear the animals all around. Spiders hunkered in the grass, I heard ravens over the sounds of cars and trucks on 101, and I saw a crippled seagull standing on one leg in the parking lot. His other foot was curled and useless. Sparrows hopped beneath cars.

Life is everywhere, even in cities. Even in cities we can see creatures who are still wild and free, who can remind us that not all creatures are slaves. There are parks, there are alleyways, there are vacant lots, there are streams, rivers, and ponds, there are birds, there are insects. This culture has polluted and harmed so much land that it sometimes becomes easy to think of unspoiled places as sacred and polluted places as sacrifice zones. But the truth is that all places are sacred. Beneath the pavement life is still there, waiting for us to remember. Or if we fail to remember, waiting for us to die off. In either case, life persists, even in seemingly barren places. Never forget that.

"But," I hear you again, "bumblebees and seagulls are boring. My child wants exciting animals."

I'm not sure how watching an insane bear or a drowsy lion or a tiger who paces and paces on concrete is more exciting than seeing wild creatures flying, hopping, crawling: doing what wild creatures do. Why are the animals at home so much less worthy? Is it because these others are from far away, and therefore become "a symbolic representation of the conquest of all distant and exotic lands"? Is it because the local animals are not in cages, and therefore not under our control?

I've known people—and perhaps this pertains to the same point—who took their children to zoos to see animals, and then came home and poisoned pigeons. I've also known people who bought their children glassed-in ant-farms, then stopped at the hardware store to buy some Raid.

Perhaps taking children to zoos to see the shells of bears when bears once walked free on this same land is to yet again teach them the wrong lesson. Perhaps if children wish to see grizzly bears we should tell them the truth: "This culture massacres them and destroys their habitat. You cannot see grizzly bears because members of this culture choose this way of life over the health of their landbase." Perhaps this would be a good time to teach your child about the consequences of destructive behaviors: if you extirpate species, you won't be able to enter into relationships with them. Perhaps this would be a good time to teach your children they can't have it all: you can't dispossess, terrorize, and destroy wild animals and expect them to welcome you. Perhaps this would be a good time to teach your children that the world and its inhabitants weren't made for humans to exploit.

IT SEEMS PRETTY CLEAR TO ME that if you want your children to see larger animals, then you need to live in such a way that those larger animals want to see you, want to live near you. Work to give them habitat (real habitat, not HABITAT™). Work to make yourself worthy of their presence.

It goes right back to the pornographic idea. Wanting to see animals when you want to see them, without being willing to work for their habitat and not get upset when they "poop all over the place," is like wanting to have sex with someone without being willing to do what is necessary for the other person to want to spend that sort of time with you. It makes no sense.

But even if you and your child work to restore habitat, work to welcome the animals home, you may not always see them when you want. And that, too, is an important lesson, perhaps more important than most. As a child I sat outside of many snake holes, willing them to come out so I could get a quick glance, but they rarely accommodated me. I'd only see them later, when walking or reading or watching some-one else. I finally learned it's not nice to look at someone who does not want to be looked at. It's like in William Faulkner's story "The Bear", in which everyone wants to see the big old bear, but the bear never presents himself until the main character leaves behind his watch, his compass, his gun, and then he gets lost. Only then does he see the bear.[111]

And who could blame the animals for hiding? Most of the apes with clothes are at this point treating those who are not *Homo supremus supremus supremus maximus* pretty poorly. If I were not an ape with clothes I would hide, too.[112] But I

can guarantee from my own experience that if you sit there long enough and ask nicely enough and work hard enough to do what is in these others best interest, in time these others will grow to trust you enough to let you know they are there. It might be subtle, like alder saplings deep in the forest chewed at forty-five degrees by aplodontia, or it might be overt, like fox poop wrapped in leaves, or the feathers and beak of a robin left behind by a hawk; or it might be unmistakable, like a big furry bear butt pressed up against your sliding glass door.

But it will be there.

The important thing in any case is to look where you live. No, it's to live where you live. It's to stop searching the world over—including the "world in a box" approach of a zoo—for some great new exotic animal experience that will somehow change your life forever, or maybe just be a spectacle novel enough to stave off the tedium for a little while. The important thing is to stop disrespecting the creatures with whom you already share a home, stop ignoring them, stop considering them not so interesting simply because they are not exotic.

I live a few miles from the ocean. Each night that the wind is right I hear sea lions barking back and forth. The wind is right almost every night. But the sound never grows old. It still thrills me to hear these others. Each winter I eagerly await the return of the frogs, whose voices grow too loud to talk over during late winter and early spring. I hear them every night. I could not fail to hear them if I tried. Yet still they move me, and I miss them when I or they are away. And when I or they are away I also miss watching the slugs who gather to scrape at the soil in one place along the path, and to eat the scat everywhere left by dogs and foxes and bears and birds and sometimes me. When I am away I miss all those others with whom I share my home, and who share their home with me. When I am away I miss my home, and I cannot wait to get back.

If when I am away I miss my home, how much moreso do you think the bear misses her home, the chimpanzee hers, the alligator his, the wolverine hers?

D[ID YOU KNOW] that many "nature" photographs and "nature" films are shot in zoos? It's much cheaper, easier, and more reliable to shoot close-ups of confined animals, and so long as the shots can be framed or photoshopped to eliminate clues like electrified wires or concrete moats, no consumers will be the wiser.

It's hard to wrap my mind around. When I look at a N[ATURE]™ photo or watch a N[ATURE]™ film I am already of course not relating to or even experiencing a wild animal, but rather consuming a simulation of one. But if the photographers or directors are presenting zoo animals as if they are free, does that mean I am now looking at a simulation of a simulation? H[ABITAT]™ is a concrete cell with tires on the floor. N[ATURE]™ is a television program filmed in prison. This echo chamber keeps getting louder and louder, making it ever more difficult to hear, to think straight, to know what is real.

And did you know that lemmings do not actually jump off of cliffs and commit suicide? The suicide story, it ends up, is a complete fabrication. Lemming populations do explode and crash, but that's based on their deeply intimate relationship with their four main predators: stoats, Arctic foxes, snowy owls, and long-tailed skuas. Lemmings are fecund, and without predation their population rises quickly. Lots of lemmings mean that the stoats, foxes, owls, and skuas have lots of food, and so they have lots of babies too. Their population rises. They eat lots of lemmings, whose population crashes, leading to a die-off of especially the stoats, who prefer lemmings to all other foods. The foxes, owls, and skuas move on to other foods, and the lemmings begin to repopulate. The cycle begins anew. This is how it has always been.

But wait! What about the mass suicides? What about that famous scene in that 1958 Disney movie *True-Life* [sic] *Adventures: White Wilderness* in which we *see* the lemmings jumping off a cliff? It was staged. As David Perlman reported in the *San Francisco Chronicle*, "Disney's camera crew was filming in Alberta where lemmings don't live. So the crew imported their own lemming extras, herded them together to simulate a mass migration and then drove them into a Hollywood-style panic to the edge of [a]…cliff, from which they leaped to their deaths en masse."[113]

Walt Disney was making a snuff film. This doesn't surprise me as much as once it might have.

Standing in the zoo, I wish I had a gun. Not just to go back in time and stop Walt Disney from ordering that film and the crew from realizing it. But to end the bear's misery. I want to break her out and take her home. Not to my home but to hers. Perhaps she would still be pacing her rectangle, but perhaps she would feel some difference in the air, in the ground beneath her feet. Perhaps she would smell some slight difference, see some slight difference. Maybe something would reach her, and she would awaken even in the slightest.

But I don't have a gun. I cannot break her out. At least not this time.

I say I'm sorry. The bear takes seven steps. I say I love you. She dips her head, takes three steps toward the front of the enclosure. I say I will put this love into action: I will get rid of zoos. She dips her head, turns, takes seven steps. I ask her what she wants. A dip, a turn, three steps. I just look at her. Another dip, another turn, another seven steps. I start to cry. Dip, turn, three steps. I tell her I will stop the culture that is destroying her home.

She stops.

She squints my direction, takes in air through her nostrils.

And then she dips her head, turns, and takes seven steps.

I wish I had a gun.

W[HEN WE SEE IT IS NOT TRUE] that zoos rescue animals, that animals are better off in zoos than in the wild, than in their own homes; when we realize that zoos do not teach us about wild animals but that instead they teach us to misperceive animals entirely, that they reinforce the flattering and absurd (as well as lonely) perception that humans are separate from and superior to all other animals; when we know that zoos are prisons; when we see that zoos are big business amusement parks attempting to pass as anything but what they are; when we say out loud that by subduing, capturing, and imprisoning those who are wild (then saying it is for their and our benefit) zoos are tangible manifestations of the mindset and processes that are killing the planet; and when we acknowledge that zoos are nightmares taking shape in concrete and steel, iron and glass, moats and electrified fences, zookeepers and their supporters fall back one more time, to their final argument: through captive breeding programs, zoos are vital to the recovery of endangered species. They cite examples of successful breeding programs: black-footed ferrets, Mongolian wild horses, red wolves, Père David's deer, European bison, Hawaiian geese, California condors, golden-headed lion tamarinds, Arabian oryx. Never mind that most of these creatures were reproduced away from public view, and never mind that the ultimate success of even most of these cases is yet to be shown. Never mind also that these are only a few photogenic species being captured and bred when the whole earth is being decimated.

Zoos are not merely beneficial to wildlife, we hear, they are necessary. And if the rhetoric surrounding the purported educational purpose of zoos was overblown, when zoo supporters speak of zoos' role in the preservation of endangered species, the language becomes positively messianic. Some book titles: *The Crowded Ark, The Welfare Ark, The Modern Ark, Lifeboat to Ararat* (which is where Noah's Ark came to land). And the text inside these books? A few not atypical examples: "The modern ark has the potential to save the planet's biodiversity, it is poised to rescue a natural world under siege."[114] And, "Bill Conway, the visionary of the zoo world, the man referred to as 'god' without a trace of sarcasm, says the mission is clear."[115] "Zoos have the weight of the world on their shoulders."[116] "No one knows exactly what the zoo of the future will look like. But with so much at stake, it is clear we desperately need zoos to help save the diversity of life. The question is not whether the world will have zoos in the future; the question is: Will the world have animals?"[117] "For the modern ark, the rains may never cease, the tide of extinction may always lap at its bow. The voyagers fighting to save the planet's biodiversity may sail on the endless sea, forever

working to hold on, to buy time,[118] to keep animals alive."[119] And finally, right to the point, "Behind the stories of zoos and captive breeding lies the assumption that we who are 'lords of the earth' and challenge the heavens must do all in our power to keep our fellow creatures alive on this planet—for it may be our last chance."[120]

There you have it: the assumption that we are "lords of the earth" is so deeply held that it is no longer even considered an assumption but rather a given that leads to the assumption underlying captive breeding in zoos.

What these authors are saying—and zookeeper after zookeeper echoes this thought—is that there is a coming extinction deluge and that zoos are the arks that will keep animals alive through this time of troubles (which may last forever). Zookeepers are the modern equivalent of Noah, the builder of the Ark.

This is a flattering notion to zookeepers. According to the Biblical story, everyone on the entire planet was wicked, except for Noah and his family. Noah, however, "was a just man and perfect in his generations, and Noah walked with God." That's not a bad place to walk if you believe in a Judeo-Christian God, that is, someone who lives far away, someone who does not reside in the land itself, someone who already gave *Homo supremus supremus supremus maximus* dominion over all beings on the planet, someone who regrets he ever made "man, and beast, and the creeping thing, and the fowls of the air," indeed, someone who hates all flesh, because "all flesh had corrupted his way upon the earth." God commanded Noah to build a big ship, upon which he was to take specimens of every creature. Then God covered the entire planet with water until everyone else was dead. After the waters receded, God told Noah to release the animals, which he did. Just to make sure Noah and his descendants understood that they were still *Homo supremus supremus supremus maximus,* God told Noah, "And the fear of you and the dread of you shall be upon every beast of the earth, and upon every fowl of the air, upon all that moveth upon the earth, and upon all the fishes of the sea; into your hand are they delivered."

The metaphor of zoos as the Ark is utterly inapt. Worse,

it is extraordinarily dangerous. First, it derives from and continues to promote the Western Judeo-Christian tradition of a sky god who does not reside here on the earth, in the soil, in the trees, in the tigers, in the catfish. A god who actually lives on this planet would never—so long as she wasn't insane—destroy her own home. We can of course say the same for humans.

Next, the ark metaphor is dangerous because it continues the tradition of domination and control—the polite term these days is "management"—that is already killing the planet. It presumes—in fact explicitly states—that humans are "lords of the earth." It presumes we are—and if you're sick of hearing this theme, just imagine how sick nonhumans are of it—separate from and superior to all other beings. It presumes that humans know better than pandas how to help pandas survive. It takes a "lord of the earth" to ask what a grizzly bear wants and come up with an answer that involves concrete and used tires, and it takes a zoo director to ask what pandas need to survive and come up with programs of confinement and artificial insemination. Pandas have been surviving extremely well, thank you very much, for thousands of times longer than civilization has been blowing out the earth. What pandas need is habitat. What pandas need is an end to civilization.

Duh.

This leads to the third problem with this metaphor, and with zoos' self-styled mission from God. In the story of Noah, there was only one ark. Zoos are too often presented in their own literature as *the* ark, *the* answer, *the* hope and salvation for wild creatures, *the* last chance. Most estimates are that somewhere in the area of one hundred to one thousand species are driven extinct by civilization every day. It's clear to anyone paying attention that the planet is undergoing ecological collapse. Given this understanding, it's clear that at the very best, zoos are not an entire ark but a slender sliver of wood that can barely float itself, much less support the weight of pandas, rhinos, elephants, and the tens of thousands of plants and animals who are extirpated entirely unnoticed by the "lords of the earth" (though noticed indeed by the landbases who mourn and miss them).

The truth is that zoos consume time and money that could be used more effectively to save more creatures by protecting habitat. Zoo supporters often argue that this comparison is unfair, because the money that goes to zoos would not otherwise go toward protecting the wild. They're right. But, as writer Mike Seidman noted sardonically, "Such is the depth of our society's commitment to conservation—not to mention our love of nature—that we will gladly donate vast sums to keep animals in elaborate cages but not to let them live wild."[121]

The fourth problem with the notion that a zoo is like an ark for saving animals is that while reproduction of endangered species in zoos is touted as crucial to the survival of wild nature, it's not even crucial to zoos. In recent years even the San Diego Zoo—considered by many to be at the forefront of "conservation"—spent more than three times as much on public relations than "in support of internationally acclaimed wildlife conservation studies conducted by CRES [Center for Reproduction of Endangered Species] scientists,"[122] in other words, on anything even remotely associated with preservation, including trips to Africa, lunches with politicians, administrative overhead, fund-raising, and so on. It's as though Noah said he was building an Ark, but spent more than three times as much of his energy telling everyone to come see his big ship (and then charging them admission).

Seidman again makes clear the priorities: "Rather than serving the cause of wild nature, these slick and polished façades, on which millions of dollars are casually spent, are really monuments to ourselves. Our real joy in them is in the creation of miniature worlds that we can contemplate and manipulate with the detached pleasure of gods. One day, through genetic engineering, we might even create animals, designing them to 'adapt' to our manufactured 'habitats' and to satisfy increasing numbers of bored and jaded urbanites."[123]

This leads to the fifth problem with the metaphor (and reality): because animals in zoos are no longer animals, animals reproduced in zoos are themselves no longer animals. Natural selection is turned on its head, as zoos select for those who are able to survive not in their habitat but in captivity: obviously if you do not survive in captivity you do not breed in captivity. Zoo breeding necessarily selects for docility, servility, a willingness to be dependent on one's keepers. It is no coincidence that these are the precise characteristics required for the majority of humans to survive civilization as well. This docility manifests at every level: ungulates bred in zoos, for example, have lower adrenaline emissions, a condition which in the wild would leave them exposed to predators. Even first-generation captive-bred birds suffer deformations so severe that, "with exceptions, the captive form has no more than a passing likeness to the wild form." Even one generation of interrupting migrations causes birds to return from migration early, to nest in adverse conditions, and so on.[124] But all of these complaints are of no importance to many zoo supporters. As longtime wildlife bureaucrat Jonathan Barzdo remarks about captive-bred animals in zoos: "Purists may even say these animals have been altered by captive breeding and are no good for the wild; but they are good enough for me."[125]

I guess that has been the point all along, hasn't it?

The sixth problem with the metaphor—and this might be the biggest problem of all—is that in the story of Noah and the Ark, the flood comes from outside. It is literally an act of God. The flood itself is entirely outside the control of Noah, who, with instructions from God (the guy with white hair, not "Bill Conway, the visionary of the zoo world") does what he can to save what God wants him to save. But that perception is entirely inaccurate. Zoos are symptoms of the same arrogant managerial ethos that is destroying the planet, which means it would be as though Noah himself were contributing to the flood and building the Ark, too. The planet is not being killed by some outside God, but rather by a culture with members who fancy themselves God, who call themselves "lords of the earth," with members who fancy they have the right to manage their landbases, and even more absurdly, the *ability* to manage their landbases without destroying them. Show me some evidence that members of this culture can manage a landbase without destroying it: you'll find none. We have plenty of examples of noncivilized peoples interacting profoundly with their landbases over tens of thousands of years or longer without destroying them. Why? Because they do not perceive themselves as separate from and superior to their non-human brothers and sisters.

Years ago I heard a story of an American Indian spiritual leader who was in a circle with a bunch of environmentalists who were drumming and singing. One of the environmentalists prayed, "Please save the spotted owl, the river otter, the peregrine falcon."

The Indian got up and whispered, "What are you doing, friend?"

"I'm praying for the animals."

"Don't pray for the animals. Pray *to* the animals." The Indian paused, then continued, "You're so arrogant, you think you're bigger than they are, right? Don't pray for the redwood. Pray that you can become as courageous as a redwood. Ask the redwood what it wants."

As it says in that self-same Bible where we read the story of Noah and his Ark, "Ask, and ye shall receive."

Ask the pandas what they want. They will tell you. The question is: are you willing to do it?

I HAVE NOTHING AGAINST using technical solutions to alleviate discrete problems, so long as we keep in mind the larger psychological and perceptual problems, so long as we realize that what we are doing is a mere stopgap.

This means I am not unalterably opposed to captive breeding programs. I have said elsewhere that I have no interest in spiritual purity. I want to live in a world with wild rhinos and tigers and red-legged frogs, and I will do whatever it takes to get there. By this I don't merely mean taking down civilization, I mean whatever it takes. This could include breeding plants and animals who are not in their habitat, if that is what the plants and animals want.

Early on in this book I noted that zookeepers asked the question, "What do grizzly bears want?" Their question, however, was a toxic mimic of a real question. It was a rhetorical device to lead themselves toward a predetermined answer. It was a lie, substituting for their real question of,

"What do grizzly bears want, given that we zookeepers will forever control their lives, and will keep them forever inside small cages we will call habitat?"

Let's ask that question again, only this time sincerely: What do grizzly bears want? And then let's ask, What do salmon want? What do spotted owls want? What do hamadryas baboons want? What do redwoods want? What do American chestnuts want?

All these lead to the next question: How do we know what they want? And when we ask those questions—what do they want, and how do we know what they want?—honestly ask those questions; ask those questions without preconceptions; ask those questions not as an excuse to incarcerate and exploit them; ask those questions not as "lords of the earth" but as friends and neighbors and loved ones; ask those questions respectfully; ask those questions of our elders; ask those questions of those who have lived on the landbases we share far longer than we have, ask those questions not just of individuals but of families, clans, communities,[126] and landbases; ask those questions as though their and our lives depend on it (because they do); we will find in time—soon, soon—that everything we've ever known will change. The din of the echo chamber will lessen, the isolation-induced hallucinations and delusions of grandeur will begin to fade. The loneliness—the devastating, soul-breaking, heart-numbing loneliness—will crack, rip, crumble, and get rushed away in a flood of newfound neighbors who have been here from the beginning, until the loneliness no longer pains, until the loneliness moves from all-consuming present to traumatic memory to the realm of cautionary tale told to future generations who literally cannot imagine how anyone could have failed to listen.

WITH ONLY A LITTLE MORE TO WRITE, I take a break and walk to the pond and notice that something is different. I freeze, scan. Then I see her, a great blue heron standing on a small rise above the far side. Her head is up and her chest is out, aimed toward the sun. Her wings are half-extended, and she stands, warming. I look at her a moment, then back away slowly, not wanting to startle her.

I smile and ask, softly, "Who are you? What do you want?"

For now, a grizzly bear still paces rectangles in a cage in a zoo. An elephant still sways hour after endless hour chained to a concrete floor. A maned wolf still strides inside an electrified fence. A giraffe still stands in a cell too small for her ever again to break into a run.

Perhaps some of these animals themselves still remember what it was like to not be a prisoner. And perhaps some were born in zoos and so have no first hand knowledge of what it was like to live free, to go where they wanted, to run, to live in a family, a community, a landbase. Perhaps they know it only from what their parents told them, who knew it only from what their parents told them, who knew it only from vague memories before their own parents were killed. Or perhaps they themselves—like so many of us—have forgotten. Perhaps for them—as for many of us—this nightmare has become the only reality they know.

They have the excuse of being behind moats, behind glass, behind walls, behind bars, behind electrified fences.

Our own confinement, our own nightmare, is perceptual and conceptual—or, more precisely, conceptual leading to perceptual—and as such we do not have their excuse. We can walk away from our own zoo, our own nightmare of self-perceived separation from and superiority to all other animals, this nightmare into which we have pulled all of these others. If this nightmare is going to have any end but death—for its individual victims, and by now for the planet—it is up to us to awaken, and having finally awakened, to end this nightmare in all its manifestations.

I type those words, then look up and away from the computer screen, out the window and into the sunlight. There is no wind. Even the bright green tips of the redwood branches are still. It's beautiful. And then I see it: a shadow the shape of a heron moving dark over the bright green. The shadow is there for only a moment, and then it's gone.

I smile.

African elephants: Samburu, Kenya

Notes

1 Hancocks, 7.

2 He also presumes that all humans are inherently destructive, citing the time-and-again discredited Pleistocene Overkill Hypothesis.

3 Hancocks, 7.

4 From the foreword to Hoage, R.J., vii.

5 For a thorough examination of this definition and of the effects of cities on their host cultures and on the landbases they destroy, see Jensen, *Endgame.*

6 Hancocks, 7.

7 Hancocks, 8.

8 Croke, 137.

9 Croke, 136.

10 Cherfas, 19.

11 Luoma, 8.

12 Luouma, 8.

13 Luoma, 8–9.

14 Luoma, 9.

15 Luoma, 9–10.

16 I can't believe that at this point I actually have to footnote this, but if you need convincing, read Jensen, *Endgame.* Or better yet, just pay attention to what's going on around you.

17 Cherfas, 19.

18 Baratay, 187.

19 Never mind that animals in zoos aren't even killed or imprisoned for food but for entertainment, and as a show of power.

20 For a thorough examination of this, see Jensen, *Endgame.*

21 Baratay, 123.

22 Baratay, 273.

23 Baratay, 124.

24 Baratay, 273.

25 Baratay, 273.

26 Batten, 131.

27 Perry, 1. He said this in the first sentence of his book, no less: "Some of our zoo cages are designed to keep animals out." The whole book, written by a former assistant director of the National Zoo, is this absurd. One sentence should suffice to leave an awful taste in your mouth: "While a number of native American species are still in danger of extinction, most of them, such as the beach meadow vole and Kaibab squirrel, were vulnerable because they were never numerous and lived in small areas." I'm not sure the salmon would agree with him, nor grizzly bears, nor sturgeon, nor spotted owls or marbled murrelets, nor many others. And check out his book's title: *The World's a Zoo.* Sigh.

28 Baratay, 273.

29 All articles by Yollin. And why the hell do they have to "eventually" find "enrichment."? If enrichment really does consist of things like cardboard boxes and paper bags, why can't someone make a quick trip to a packing store?

30 The parallelism does not escape me between Freud's pretending to ask that question about women and then answering in ways that served male domination of women, and these zookeepers pretending to ask that question about wild animals, and then answering in ways that serve civilized domination of the wild.

31 I am excluding of course such obvious counterexamples as doing field surveys for endangered species, reporting exotics who harm native species, and reporting animals who have been severely injured by automobiles to the highway patrol so someone can, not euphemistically this time, "humanely destroy" the animal.

32 Of course. It's killing the planet. It is not possible to be more insane than that.

33 "Meet the Grizzly Bears."

34 As if a "human world" exists. It's not a human world, obviously, except in the deranged minds of these narcissists. The degree to which any people believe this is a "human world" is

the degree to which they have been inculcated into this culture, and are therefore inculpated in the atrocities it commits.

35 And psychopathology.

36 Montgomery, 39.

37 Mullan, 157–158.

38 Above quotes from Mullan, 83–84.

39 Kirchshofer, citing Hediger, 9.

40 Mullan, 84. And note, significantly enough, that even in this example, instead of describing his own experience of being locked in his office, he hypothetically locks you up.

41 NOAZ ARK.

42 Jensen and Draffan, 26.

43 Mullan, 159.

44 *Animal Planet.*

45 Yollin, "Grizzlies turn into cash cows." These damn journalists simply cannot help themselves. They must disrespect the animals each chance they get, and they must attempt to convince their readers the animals enjoy their incarceration. So far as the former, the reporter makes sure to quote a six-year-old as he yells, "Hey, big fat bears." So far as the latter, the title of the second page of the article is, "Nameless bears having loads of fun."

46 Rubenstein.

47 Perry, 267.

48 Croke, 252.

49 Densmore, 172.

50 Hancocks, 252.

51 Baratay, 209.

52 Baratay, 236.

53 Batten, 22.

54 Hancocks, 148. The caption continues, "...because we don't know just what the animal is thinking. Clearly, though, such conditions are not conducive to natural behaviors, and it is safe to conclude that this must be an unhappy and stressed animal. Moreover, the conditions in which it [sic] is displayed could never elicit any sense of admiration or wonder for what [sic] is in fact an admirable and wonderful being." I love this whole quote because it reveals step-by-step one of the central mindfucks inherent in zookeeping. First, the animal is caged. Then the animal responds as many animals—including human animals—do to confinement. Then we are told that our natural empathic response to this creature is a misinterpretation, implying that we should not trust our own empathy. Then having made clear that we are prone to misinterpret behavior, the expert gives his opinion, which in this case kind of agrees with ours, except that he uses bigger words—" not conducive to natural behaviors"—implying greater intelligence and less emotionality than we have, and most importantly no longer speaks of the call to action the macaque was clearly making (which the zookeeper would say we were misinterpreting): the "mute appeal for help and consolation from its [sic] enforced isolation." Having, the zookeeper hopes, dissuaded us from helping or consoling this poor creature, the zookeeper can then turn our impulse to action into its toxic mimic and we can safely step back, knowing that the intrepid zookeeper is going to work hard to improve "the conditions in which it [sic] is displayed" so that "it" can "elicit" in us not pity or sorrow but "a sense of admiration or wonder." It's a brilliant piece of rhetoric.

55 Baratay, 19.

56 Berger, 19.

57 Rothfels, 21, citing Thomas, 277.

58 Baratay, 115.

59 Baratay, 118.

60 Baratay, 114.

61 Rothfels, 60.

62 Cherfas, 19.

63 Rothfels, 61.

64 Rothfels, 61.

65 Note that other accounts suggest that only one of the young elephants survived; Rothfels, 218.

66 Rothfels, 61–62.

67 Rothfels, 62.

68 Rothfels, 62.

69 Rothfels, 64.

70 "Between 1866 and 1886, Carl Hagenbeck exported [from only the port of Marseilles] around seven hundred leopards, one thousand lions and four hundred tigers, one thousand bears, eight hundred hyenas, three hundred elephants, Seventy rhinoceroses from India, Java, and Sumatra and nine from Africa, three hundred camels, one hundred fifty giraffes, six hundred antelopes, tens of thousands of monkeys, thousands of crocodiles, boas, and pythons (in which his firm specialized) and substantially more than one hundred thousand birds." [Baratay, 118]. Remember, this was only his exports from one port for only one portion of his career, and recall further the incredibly high mortality at every point both preceding and following this in the supply chain.

71 Rothfels, 67.

72 Note the utter disinterest in the experience of the nonhuman. Here, by someone else, is an account of how dolphins are often caught, after having been chased to exhaustion by motorboats: "Pulling up the nets, perhaps the first victims are found; those dolphins which [sic] have become entangled and drowned, those that [sic] have injured themselves trying to escape, sometimes tearing off a flipper as they thrash around in panic. Then comes the strenuous effort of heaving the selected animals on board.... Many a dolphin has to be thrown back into the water, paralyzed, after its spine has been broken. The boats then speed back to land, leaving the dolphin school with its own unseen, unrecognized bereavement, the sucklings will die without their mothers to nurse them, the injured which [sic] are held aloft by their companions, perhaps for days until they take their last breath." [Margodt, 8]

73 Kirchshofer 215–216, citing Hermann, Jr.

74 Rothfels, 218.

75 Croke, 216.

76 Batten, 27.

77 Baratay and Hardouin-Fugier, 279.

78 Baratay and Hardouin-Fugier, 279.

79 Batten, 28–29.

80 Baratay and Hardouin-Fugier, 279.

81 Batten, 31.

82 Batten, 32.

83 Batten, 33.

84 Baratay and Hardouin-Fugier, 280.

85 Note that while some indigenous cultures have tortured or ritually caged some animals, the overwhelming majority have not, and that even those cultures which have committed these acts have in no way rivaled especially this civilization for its systematic torture, enslavement, imprisonment, and extirpation of nonhumans and the wild.

86 Oh, sorry, a HABITAT™.

87 Have you noticed that bears in the wild don't pay quite so much attention to bags and boxes? Maybe they do in a cage because it relieves the tedium even the tiniest bit.

88 Whew! That was a close one. It's a good thing we explained away destroying the natural world as a biological imperative or we might actually have to do something to stop it!

89 Kirby.

90 McNeil

91 Jensen, *Listening to the Land*, 61.

92 Livingston, 94–95.

93 Hancocks, 173.

94 I made up the names, not the prices.

95 It was Upton Sinclair, by the way.

96 As we talked, we stood in the lobby of a hotel. In front of us was an ornate bird cage hand carved in the shape of a mansion. "No matter the fine craft that went into this," he said, "you can't disguise the fact that it's a cage." The subtlest movement of his head and his hand made clear he meant both the smaller structure in front of us and the larger structures surrounding us.

97 Baratay, 205.

98 Baratay 207–208.

99 Jensen, "Where the Buffalo Go."

100 Shepard, *The Only World We've Got*, 73; 74–75.

101 Jensen, *Listening to the Land*, 251.

102 Shepard, Paul, *Coming Home to the Pleistocene*, 39.

103   Shepard, *The Only World We've Got*, i.

104   Jensen, *Listening to the Land*, 257.

105   Shepard, *Coming Home to the Pleistocene*, 57.

106   Shepard, *Coming Home to the Pleistocene*, 41.

107   And just for grins, look up "wisdom" in the index of your average science textbook: I'll bet you a nickel it's not there.

108   Jensen, "Where the Buffalo Go."

109   Often having passed through confusion on the way.

110   Campbell, Joseph, 5.

111   I love that metaphor so much it makes me almost want to forgive him for writing *The Sound and the Fury*. Almost.

112   I am an ape with clothes, and sometimes I still want to hide.

113   Perlman,

114   Croke, 237.

115   Croke, 243.

116   Croke, 243.

117   Croke, 252.

118   If they really believe it's forever, for what are they buying time? And if they don't, why aren't they trying to stop the deluge?

119   Croke, 254.

120   Campbell, Sheldon, xiv.

121   Seidman, 68–69.

122   Croke, 244.

123   Seidman, 68.

124   Baratay and Hardouin-Fugier, 273–274.

125   Mullan, 158.

126   "Scientists highlight fish 'intelligence.'" Note that even here, the journalist who came up with the headline is so insecure about human intelligence and so sure that fish cannot be intelligent that he or she places quotes around the word intelligence. It's extraordinary how deeply held is this arrogance. (You do know, don't you, that many species of fish form extensive and fluid social groups, and that fish are, as now even scientists have been forced to acknowledge, "regarded as steeped in social intelligence, pursuing Machiavellian strategies of manipulation, punishment and reconciliation, exhibiting stable cultural traditions, and co-operating to inspect predators and catch food".)

Bibliography

"Animal Planet: From India's famed camel fair to Indonesia's fierce Komodo dragons—all the world's a zoo," *San Francisco Chronicle,* November 28, 2004, F1, F4.

Baratay, Eric, and Elisabeth Hardouin-Fugier, *Zoo: A History of Zoological Gardens in the West,* Reaktion Books, London, 2002.

Batten, Peter, *Living Trophies,* Thomas Y. Crowell, New York, 1976.

Berger, John, "Why Look At Animals," in *About Looking,* Pantheon, New York, 1980.

Campbell, Joseph, *The Masks of God, Volume IV: Creative Mythology,* Penguin, New York, 1968.

Campbell, Sheldon, *Lifeboats to Ararat,* New York Times Book Company, New York, 1978.

Croke, Vicki, *The Modern Ark: The Story of Zoos: Past, Present and Future,* Scribner, New York, 1997.

Densmore, Frances, *Teton Sioux Music,* Bulletin 61, Bureau of American Ethnology, Smithsonian Institution, 1918, p. 172.

Hancocks, David, *A Different Nature: The Paradoxical World of Zoos and Their Uncertain Future,* University of California Press, Berkeley, 2001.

Hoage, R.J., and William A. Deiss, with a foreward by Michael H. Robinson, *New Worlds, New Animals: From Menagerie to Zoological Park in the Nineteenth Century,* Johns Hopkins University Press, Baltimore, 1996.

Jensen, Derrick, Endgame, *Volume 1: The Problem of Civilization,* and *Endgame, Volume 2: Resistance,* Seven Stories Press, New York, 2006.

Jensen, Derrick, *Listening to the Land: Conversations About Nature, Culture, and Eros,* Chelsea Green, White River Junction, 2004.

Jensen, Derrick, "Where the Buffalo Go: How Science Ignores the Living World: An Interview with Vine Deloria," *The Sun,* July, 2000.

Jensen, Derrick, and George Draffan, *Welcome to the Machine: Science, Surveillance, and the Culture of Control,* Chelsea Green, White River Junction, 2004.

Kirby, Alex, "Fish do feel pain, scientists say," *BBC News,* April 30, 2004, <http://news.bbc.co.uk/2/hi/science/nature/2983045.stm> (accessed May 12, 2003).

Kirchshofer, Rosl, editor, *The World of Zoos: A Survey and Gazetteer,* Viking, New York, 1968.

Livingston, John A., *The Fallacy of Wildlife Conservation,* McClelland & Stewart, Toronto, 1981.

Luoma, Jon R., *A Crowded Ark,* Houghton Mifflin, Boston, 1987.

Margodt, Koen, *The Welfare Ark: Suggestions for a Renewed Policy in Zoos,* VUB University Press, Brussels, 2000.

McNeil, Donald G., "Videos Cited in Calling Kosher Slaughterhouse Inhumane," *The New York Times,* December 1, 2004, <http://www.nytimes.com/2004/12/01/national/01kosher.html> (accessed December 2, 2004).

"Meet The Grizzly Bears," *San Francisco Chronicle,* E20.

Mullan, Bob, and Garry Marvin, *Zoo Culture: The Book About Watching People Watch Animals,* second edition, University of Illinois Press, Urbana, 1999.

NOAZ ARK, <http://www.noazark.org/> (accessed November 24, 2004).

Perlman, David, "Lemmings' death wish nothing but a tale—told by Disney: Predators, not mass suicide, account for Arctic rodents' population cycles, study finds," *San Francisco Chronicle,* October 31, 2003.

Perry, John, *The World's a Zoo,* Dodd, Mead & Company, New York, 1969.

Rothfels, Nigel, *Savages and Beasts: The Birth of the Modern Zoo,* Johns Hopkins, Baltimore, 2002.

Rubenstein, Steve, "Shark hits 100th day at grateful aquarium: Great White adds to survival record—and to gross receipts," *San Francisco Chronicle,* December 23, 2004, B1, B3.

"Scientists highlight fish 'intelligence': Fish are socially intelligent creatures who do not deserve their reputation as the dim-wits of the animal kingdom, according to a group of leading scientists," *BBCNews,* 8/31/2003, <http://news.bbc.co.uk/2/hi/uk_news/

england/west_yorkshire/3189941.stm> (accessed December 25, 2004).

Seidman, Mike, "Zoos and the Psychology of Extinction," *Wild Earth,* Winter 1992/93, 64–69.

Shepard, Paul, *Coming Home to the Pleistocene,* Island Press, Covelo, CA, 1998.

Shepard, Paul, *The Only World We've Got: A Paul Shepard Reader,* Sierra Club Books, San Francisco, 1996.

Thomas, Keith, *Man and the Natural World: A History of the Modern Sensibility,* Pantheon, New York, 1983.

Yollin, Patricia, "Bad girls have a good day as they go outside at zoo: Montana grizzlies entertain public, astound keepers," *San Francisco Chronicle,* November 18, 2004, B1, <http://sfgate.com/cgibin/article.cgi?f=/c/a/2004/11/18/BAG269T4AC49.DTL> (accessed November 19, 2004).

Yollin, Patricia, "Grizzlies turn into cash cows: Free public contest is dumped in favor of getting big bucks from highest bidder—corporate or individual," *San Francisco Chronicle,* April 16, 2005, A1, A8.

Yollin, Patricia, "Mischievous grizzly cubs to be adopted by S.F. Zoo: Montana planned to kill 2 orphan bears," *San Francisco Chronicle,* September 30, 2004, <http://www.sfgate.com/cgibin/article.cgi?file=/c/a/2004/09/30/MNG9U91AMS1.DTL> (accessed November 19, 2004).

Yollin, Patricia, "Nice Grizzly Grotto Poses a Bear of a Problem," *San Francisco Chronicle,* November 15, 2004, A1, <http://www.sfgate.com/cgibin/article.cgi?file=/chronicle/archive/2004/11/15/MNGKA9RNFE1.DTL> (accessed November 19, 2004).

Yollin, Patricia, "Rowdy gals face a tamer S.F. lifestyle: After escaping death, sister grizzlies are en route to zoo," *San Francisco Chronicle,* October 3, 2004.

Photographer's Note

The majority of the photographs in this book were taken at what are considered to be the finest zoos in this country. In the United States alone, some 10,000 substandard zoos exist in which the incarcerates' living conditions are squalid and grim. Therefore, the animals in these photographs are representatives of a vast number of others who are not included here. Two individuals, the Przewalski's wild horse (or Mongolian wild horse) and the dromedary (Arabian, Egyptian, or North African camel), stand here for their entire species, which no longer live wild. The present-day dromedary is entirely domesticated. Since the 1990s, attempts have been made to reintroduce the Mongolian horse to the steppes (a geographic area that is itself endangered); a 2005 census lists 248 free-ranging horses, all descended from captive animals. Many zoos justify the enormous effort and expense of confining exotic individuals as a way to save species from extinction. Efforts at reintroduction often fail because the "wild" and its myriad support systems are gone. Despite instances of near extinction, the misery of any animal's lifelong confinement is intolerable and inherently unjustifiable.

Acknowledgments

This book is dedicated to Lou Grassi, my husband and ever my optionaire, and to the memory of my extraordinary mother, Virginia Tweedy Holmes, never a fan of zoos. For their continued encouragement, good humor, and support through the years, I want to thank my friends Judith Anderson, Christopher Collins Lee, Cynthia Insolio Benn, Katherine Mindlin Reinleitner, Dale Roberts, Louise Gikow, Barbara Kolsun, Julie Reich, Anita Chernewski, Jerry Alpern, Beryl Goldberg, the Howell family, Carlton Willers, Stephen Weislogel, Irene Vandermolen, Anne Ranson, Abby Ripley, Sydney Hamburger, Margaret Bassett, Katherine Minott, Jeanie Linn, and Gina Duclayan, and my beloved equestrian cousin, Larry Bolen. I thank Julie Burke for introducing me to Derrick Jensen and for her work on an early version of this book, our agent, Anthony Arnove, and Mike Miller for his beautiful, balanced layout design. I am grateful beyond words to Derrick for giving me this opportunity to join my photographs with his powerful essay on behalf of the animals and to our publishers, Diane Leigh and Marilee Geyer, who have enabled the two of us to reach outward to foster awareness of the insanity of incarcerating animals for human entertainment and profit.

The photographs in this book were taken at the Central Park Zoo, New York City; Como Park Zoo, Minneapolis, Minnesota; Jersey Wildlife Preservation Trust, Channel Islands, United Kingdom; The National Zoo, Washington, DC; New York Zoological Society (Wildlife Conservation Society), Bronx, New York; Philadelphia Zoo, Philadelphia, Pennsylvania; Prospect Park Zoo, Brooklyn, New York; Queens Wildlife Center, Flushing, New York; Reid Park Zoo, Tucson, Arizona; San Diego Zoo, San Diego, California; Staten Island Zoo, New York; Toledo Zoo, Toledo, Ohio; and Zoo Atlanta, Atlanta, Georgia.

Przewalski's wild horse (Mongolian wild horse, Asiatic wild horse, Takhi), *Equus caballus przewalskii:* Extinct in the wild after 1968.

A Note from the Publisher

This book was turned down by numerous commercial publishers. Because we have all been taught for decades—for our entire lifetimes—that zoos are good and necessary places, making a case otherwise is not a popular, or "marketable," stand. And so it falls to a small, non-profit organization to send this voice out into the world.

Although many of the animals in this book are mammals—those animals in whom, looking into their eyes, we can recognize suffering—it bears remembering that zoos hold captive all manner of species, and that each and every one of these animals suffers in his or her own unique way, even if we can't readily see it.

And, although many zoos would tell us that their "habitats" for the animals have been greatly improved throughout the years, and that some of the photos in this book are not reflective of that, know that there are zoos and aquariums from one end of this country to the other (and in other countries) with horrible conditions, holding animals who suffer tremendously. In any case, the only important question is not the quality of the conditions in which they are held captive, but whether they should be held captive at all.

For more information on the massive underground trade in "exotic" animals, we recommend the amazing book, *Animal Underworld: Inside America's Black Market for Rare and Exotic Species,* by Alan Green, published by the Center for Public Integrity. You will never look at zoos in the same way again.

We send you our thanks for reading *Thought to Exist in the Wild*. We are working to distribute it widely, and to get it on the shelves of public and university libraries where inquiring minds can be presented with an alternative view of zoos. If you would like to help expand the voice created by this book, our Giving Package offers five copies at a discounted price to donate to libraries, share with family and friends, send to media, and give as gifts. For more information, visit www.NoVoiceUnheard.org.

Acknowledgments

This book was made possible with the vision and generous support of: Barbara J. Goodrich, Robin S. Rawls, Katherine Mindlin Reinleitner, Stephen Colley, Lisa Lewis, Ben Lewis, Diane Hamelin, Margaret Kupps, Joan M. Cummings, Meryl Lewin, Nell S. Cliff, Patrick Welch & Debbie Sitka, Patsy Volpe, Lorraine Hoge, Peggy Pace, Kristin White Del Rosso, Sam Burkhardt, Barbara Beyer-Altieri, Mary Beth Brown, Linda Sullivan, John & Pepper Hall, Lori A. Koch, Monique Leduc, Mary Sweeley Castro, Wendy Hyatt, Al French, Katarina Donohue, Virginia Kallianes, Amy Buriss, Julie Mascavage.

Gratitude and thanks to Davida Breier, Theresa Noll, Lisa Rudin, Bill Maher, Andy Hurley, Stephen Mitchell, Frank Noelker, Julie Burke, Anthony Arnove, Tom Campbell & The Guacamole Fund, Mike Miller–Prism Photographics, David Wing–Art and Development, Carol Cuminale, JP Novic, Windi Wojdak, Kathy Ninneman, Bob Geyer, and Kevin.

As always, for the animals

ALL OUR RELATIONS

About the Publisher

No Voice Unheard is a non-profit, tax exempt 501(c)3 organization dedicated to promoting compassion and respect for all living beings and the planet we share. We generate exposure, education, advocacy, and action in support of our mission, and have carved out a niche as an independent publisher of distinctive books that are cutting-edge in their content and presentation. Our books illuminate important social issues, creating unique voices on behalf of those who are unseen, ignored or disregarded by society.

No Voice Unheard was founded by the authors of *One at a Time: A Week in an American Animal Shelter,* after commercial publishers told them the book was too graphic to be marketable. Now in a third printing, the book resides on hundreds of public and university library shelves, serves as a college course book, and is used by individuals, shelters, and rescue groups across the country to educate their communities about this nation's homeless animal tragedy. Thousands of copies are in circulation, touching hearts and changing minds.

Donations to No Voice Unheard are tax deductible. Your contribution will help underwrite the expenses associated with producing our books, so that proceeds from their sales can be used for educational outreach programs and events.

For more information, visit: www.NoVoiceUnheard.org

NO VOICE UNHEARD

P. O. Box 4171
Santa Cruz, California 95063
(831) 440-9574
(831) 479-3225 fax
info@novoiceunheard.org

No Voice Unheard books are distributed by
Biblio Book Distribution – (800) 462-6420